TIME MANAGEMENT TIPS for FARMERS

Sustainable Farmers Share Tips For Taming The To-Do List

CAROLINE OWENS

outskirts press

The opinions expressed in this manuscript are solely the opinions of the author and do not represent the opinions or thoughts of the publisher. The author has represented and warranted full ownership and/or legal right to publish all the materials in this book.

Time Management Tips for Farmers
Sustainable Farmers Share Tips For Taming The To-Do List
All Rights Reserved.
Copyright © 2016 Caroline Owens
v3.0

Cover Photo © 2016 Caroline Owens. All rights reserved - used with permission.
Original cover art created by Kristi Stoyko.

This book may not be reproduced, transmitted, or stored in whole or in part by any means, including graphic, electronic, or mechanical without the express written consent of the publisher except in the case of brief quotations embodied in critical articles and reviews.

Outskirts Press, Inc.
http://www.outskirtspress.com

ISBN: 978-1-4787-7765-6

Outskirts Press and the "OP" logo are trademarks belonging to Outskirts Press, Inc.

PRINTED IN THE UNITED STATES OF AMERICA

This book is dedicated to my husband David, and to our awesome children Kyle, Kevin, and Melissa.

Table of Contents

WHY THIS BOOK?..I
BERRY FIELDS FARM..1
    LABOR STRATEGY 2
    USE OF TECHNOLOGY 2
    TIME MANAGEMENT TIP: WEEKLY MASTER LIST 3
    TIME MANAGEMENT TIP: WHO NEEDS HELP
        AND WHEN?..4
    ADVICE FOR NEW FARMERS......................................4
BLUE ROOSTER FARM..5
    MOSTLY FAMILY LABOR 5
    TIME MANAGEMENT TIP: PROFESSIONAL ADVICE 6
    YES TO TECHNOLOGY 6
    PLANNING STYLES 7
    ADVICE FOR NEW FARMERS......................................7
FORKS FARM 9
    LABOR SITUATION..10
    FACTORS THAT CHANGE THE DAILY PLAN 10
    USE OF TECHNOLOGY 11
    TIME MANAGEMENT TIP: MASTER CALENDAR 11
    TIME MANAGEMENT TIP: NO NAGGIN'....................12
    ADVICE FOR NEW FARMERS....................................13
HAMEAU FARM 14
    LABOR 14
    ORGANIZING THE DAYS..15
    GOOD OLD-FASHIONED NOTEBOOK 15
    SEASONAL CHANGES 16

- ADVICE FOR NEW FARMERS...16
- HERRING'S GREEN GRASS FARM 18
  - LABOR 18
  - MORNING PLANS AND PAPER CALENDARS..............19
  - SOCIAL MEDIA UTILIZATION 19
  - ADMINISTRATIVE TIME 20
  - SUDDEN CHANGES OF PLAN 20
  - SEASONALITY..20
  - FORMAL TIME MANAGEMENT TRAINING.................20
  - ADVICE FOR NEW FARMERS...21
- JUJO ACRES 23
  - LABOR 23
  - ORGANIZING THE DAYS...24
  - ADVICE TO NEW FARMERS 24
  - CLOSING THOUGHTS 25
- THE WHY 26
- LE-ARA FARMS..28
  - FAMILY LABOR ONLY 28
  - DIVIDE AND CONQUER PAPERWORK......................29
  - FORWARD-PLANNING SAVES TIME...........................29
  - TYPICAL DAY 30
  - ADVICE FOR NEW FARMERS...30
- MYSTIC SPRINGS FARM 31
  - LABOR SITUATION..32
  - TIME MANAGEMENT TIP:
    - DIVIDE AND CONQUER 32
  - FACTORS THAT CHANGE THE DAILY PLAN..............33
  - USE OF TECHNOLOGY 34
  - ADVICE FOR NEW FARMERS...34

- NEW MORNING FARM 35
  - LABOR 35
  - EVOLUTION IN SCALE 36
  - CREW MEETING STARTS THE DAY 37
  - TECHNOLOGY 37
  - ADVICE FOR NEW FARMERS 37
- ONE STRAW FARM 39
  - LABOR STRATEGY 39
  - TECHNOLOGY 41
  - SEASONALITY 41
  - PAPERWORK 41
  - OUTSOURCING 41
  - ADVICE FOR NEW FARMERS 42
- OVER THE MOON FARM 43
  - LABOR 43
  - PAPERWORK UNDER COVER OF DARKNESS 44
  - WEEKLY PLAN 44
  - WEATHER REPORT BEGINS THE DAY 45
  - VISITS AND FARM TOURS 45
  - TIME MANAGEMENT TRAINING 45
  - ADVICE FOR NEW FARMERS 46
- OWENS FARM 48
  - THE ONE THING RULE 49
  - MONTHLY PLANNING SESSION 50
  - PAPERWORK BEFORE DAWN 52
  - ADVICE FOR NEW FARMERS 52
- PAINTED HAND FARM 53
  - LABOR STRATEGY 53
  - USE OF TECHNOLOGY 54
  - TIME MANAGEMENT TIP: PHYSICAL LAYOUT 54

TIME MANAGEMENT TIP: VOLUNTEER CAREFULLY .. 55
TIME MANAGEMENT TIP: JOURNAL-STYLE
  TO-DO LIST 55
  ADVICE FOR NEW FARMERS 56
POLYFACE FARM Inc. 57
  THE FACES BEHIND POLYFACE 58
  JUST MATILDA AND ME DOWN ON THE FARM 58
  UGH, PROFITS 59
  TIME AND MOTION STUDIES 59
  DAY-TO-DAY LIFE AT POLYFACE 60
  CONTROLLING CHORES 60
  ADVICE FOR NEW FARMERS 61
PATCHWORK FARM & GREENHOUSE 62
  LABOR 62
  DIVIDE AND CONQUER 63
  ORGANIZING THE DAY 63
  TECHNOLOGY 64
  EMPLOYEE RETENTION 64
  FAMILY TIME 64
  ADVICE FOR NEW FARMERS 65
PURELY FARM 66
  LABOR 66
  SOLO LIVESTOCK MANAGEMENT 68
  TECHNOLOGY 68
  ADVICE FOR NEW FARMERS 69
QUIET CREEK HERB FARM AND SCHOOL
  OF COUNTRY LIVING 71
  LABOR STRATEGY 72
  SEASONAL SEGMENTATION 72
  SPREAD OUT SPRING PLANTING 73

THE COLOR-CODED CHALKBOARD 74
BALANCING PUBLIC AND PERSONAL TIME 74
USE OF TECHNOLOGY 74
ADVICE FOR NEW FARMERS 75
SPIRAL PATH FARM 76
LABOR 76
CSA SOFTWARE SAVES THE DAY 78
INVESTMENT IN EFFICIENCY 78
CONSTANT FLOW OF COMMUNICATION 79
ORGANIZING THE DAYS 79
VISITOR MANAGEMENT 80
ADVICE FOR NEW FARMERS 80
STEAM VALLEY FIBER FARM 82
LABOR STRATEGY 83
USE OF TECHNOLOGY 84
TIME MANAGEMENT TIP: WEEKLY PLAN 84
TIME MANAGEMENT TIP:
    ON-SITE PASTURE RECORDS 84
TIME MANAGEMENT TIP:
    FIXED CHORE PATTERNS 85
ADVICE FOR NEW FARMERS 85
TEWKSBURY GRACE FARM 87
FREEDOM FROM MACHINERY 87
KEEPING TECHNOLOGY IN ITS PLACE 88
SAVING TIME BY STAYING HOME 88
DAILY, WEEKLY, SEASONAL SCHEDULES 89
INVESTING IN QUALITY 90
ADVICE FOR NEW FARMERS 90
STRYKER FARM 92
LABOR 92

NUMBERED TO DO LIST 93
STRYKER FARM TECHNOLOGY 93
ADVICE FOR NEW FARMERS 94
WYNNORR FARM 95
    LABOR STRATEGY 96
    USE OF TECHNOLOGY 97
    CONSISTENT SCHEDULES 97
    WHAT'S THE MOST IMPORTANT THING
        RIGHT NOW? 98
    PREVIOUS TIME MANAGEMENT EXPERIENCE 98
    ADVICE FOR NEW FARMERS 99
THE CONNECTION BETWEEN HOLISTIC
    MANAGEMENT AND TIME MANAGEMENT 101
    THE PRINCIPLES 102
    THE PRACTICES 104
    PRACTICE ONE—DEFINE WHAT YOU MANAGE 104
    PRACTICE TWO—STATE WHAT YOU WANT 105
    PRACTICE THREE—AIM FOR HEALTHY SOIL 106
    PRACTICE FOUR—CONSIDER ALL TOOLS
        AVAILABLE 106
    PRACTICE FIVE—TEST YOUR DECISIONS 107
MAXIMIZE OUTREACH, MINIMIZE TIME WITH A WEEKLY
    COMMUNICATION SCHEDULE 110
    PART 1: THE THREE PIECES OF CONTENT YOU NEED
        TO CREATE EACH WEEK 111
    PART 2: REACH PEOPLE WHERE THEY ARE 114
    PART 3: SCHEDULE, TIMING, AND TOOLS: 119

WHY THIS BOOK?

By the age of thirty-something, I had successfully managed my career in the corporate world with a paper-based time management system. The core principal involved assigning letters to tasks in a daily calendar. An "A" was high priority and urgent, "B" somewhat less so, and "C" neither important nor time-sensitive. The list was reviewed and reprioritized on an ongoing basis. This system worked very well in an office environment with clearly defined chains of command and support staff.

And then my husband and I bought a 112-acre farm. In July.

We were immediately faced with the prospect of winterizing a rickety old farmhouse, acquiring livestock, shoring up infrastructure, settling our children into school, and launching our direct meat business from ground zero. We quickly exceeded the limitations of our time management system.

What do you do when everything is an "A"? What do you do when working your hardest is not good enough? What do you do when your dream threatens to become a nightmare? Burn-out was looking us squarely in the face. We needed a new way to tackle the To Do list. David and I did figure out a better way to manage our work/life balance, and our farm flourished.

Flash forward several years. We became active members of Pennsylvania Association for Sustainable Agriculture (PASA) and also found great satisfaction in offering workshops on livestock production. As a result, we came to know many farmers. I was struck by an oft-repeated and familiar theme. New farmers would find themselves insanely busy and perpetually overloaded. They assumed that things would naturally settle down "once the business got off the ground". But as time passed, they would get even busier. Something had to change. Determined to succeed, they would figure out specific strategies to improve their situation and allow them to move forward.

Sharing information is one of the basic tenets of PASA. From weed control to marketing savvy, this organization excels at bringing producers together to share tips and techniques. Why not, I thought, use the same approach to time management? If individual farms are coming up with creative strategies for saving their sanity, why not share these ideas so everyone doesn't have to reinvent the same wheel?

And thus was conceived the concept for this book. It was only natural that the farmers I turned to were those in the PASA community. Not surprisingly, they embraced the idea and were willing to share their thoughts on this rather personal subject. I extend a heartfelt thank you to all the producers in this book, and for all that PASA has done in being there for my farm and family.

BERRY FIELDS FARM

New Albany, Pennsylvania
CHARLIE AND BARBARA GERLACH

Nestled on 51 scenic acres in the Endless Mountains of northeast Pennsylvania, Berry Fields is an organic farm offering lodging and dining for overnight guests. Charlie and Barbara are the sole proprietors. With the help of a greenhouse and hoophouse, they grow a large organic garden which supplies produce for themselves, their on-farm restaurant, a CSA, and a summer farmers' market. A mountainside orchard produces heritage pears and apples. The farm's namesake is the extensive blueberry patch which provides fruit for all their customers plus a seasonal pick-your-own operation.

Home-raised meats and eggs are an important part of the picture. Charlie and Barbara raise Hereford cattle, Tamworth pigs, and Boer goats. They also maintain a flock of laying hens and ducks, and raise an annual batch of turkeys. The animals and poultry contribute to the farm in multiple ways. The meat is used in the restaurant and offered for sale in the farm store. Caring for the animals is part of the appeal for overnight guests, who participate in daily chores. The farm offers lodging in two beautifully decorated units: a guesthouse for

2-10 people, and a smaller apartment. Hand-in-hand with the overnight lodging is an on-farm restaurant. Here, Barbara and Charlie serve Saturday evening dinners and Sunday brunches made with farm-fresh ingredients. No cook is hired: Charlie and Barbara handle the entire meal from prep to serving to clean-up.

Tying everything together is the on-farm retail store featuring Berry Fields' own produce and meats plus other local farms' products such as cheese, honey, maple syrup, baked goods and crafts.

LABOR STRATEGY

Barbara and Charlie have owned this farm for 11 years, doing most of the work themselves with occasional hired help. For the first few years, there was a young neighbor always willing to pitch in. Just about the time he grew up and left home, Charlie and Barbara's grandson enthusiastically filled the void. At the time of this writing, he had "grown and flown" and labor was once again a problem. Charlie and Barbara were initiating plans to bring on summer interns.

USE OF TECHNOLOGY

Cell phones and a website are the only two technologies used at Berry Fields Farm. The website is their most important marketing tool. Cell phones allow Charlie and Barbara to be immediately available to guests while working around the farm.

TIME MANAGEMENT TIP: WEEKLY MASTER LIST

Charlie and Barbara bring to the farm a unique perspective in time management. Before Berry Fields, the couple owned their own business in residential remodeling. Success in this field demands organizational and time management skills of the highest level. The tasks and subcontractors must be properly sequenced and monitored to complete a building project on time and on budget. Charlie had extensive formal training in time management to support this aspect of the business. This background is reflected in how Barbara and Charlie work together at Berry Fields. At the beginning of each week, they craft a single, prioritized list of what needs to be done. This master list is edited and added to as the week progresses.

The morning ritual in the Gerlach household includes a review of the list and creation of a plan for the day. The two most critical decisions are a) what are the priorities? and b) who needs help and when?

With so many parallel enterprises, prioritizing can be a challenge. Even after lengthy analysis, Charlie and Barbara don't always agree on what's most important. The acid test is, "what will hurt the business most if we don't get it done?" Some days they simply agree to disagree, and each tackles their own most important project.

"The list is a mess by the end of the week", says Barbara. "That's when I update it as to what has been done and what has been added going into the new week. That way we don't forget about projects or new ideas, and we get a sense of satisfaction over what's been done".

TIME MANAGEMENT TIP: WHO NEEDS HELP AND WHEN?

The other critical element of the breakfast discussion is "who needs help, and when". With just the two of them working on the farm, Charlie and Barbara have to be very judicious in their use of time. Some tasks are more efficiently done by one person. Others are best done with two. Transplanting, for example, takes less than half the time with two people than with one. If they can figure out in the morning who will need help and when, they can each plan their day. And yes—there are many times when they each need each other's help at the same time. That's when their lifetime of negotiation skills comes into play.

ADVICE FOR NEW FARMERS

The business end of your farm is as important as the nuts and bolts of production. Good management is the key to being financially sustainable as well as ecologically sustainable at farming.

"Don't expect to be able to get everything on your list done every day," observes Barbara. "This was the hardest adjustment for me when we bought the farm." In her prior business life, she prided herself on completing her daily office tasks, and was professionally rewarded for her competence. Naturally, she expected to transfer this model of success to her budding new farm business. It took her a full year of stress to accept the new reality. "I learned to find joy in the doing, not the having done", she concludes.

BLUE ROOSTER FARM

Waterford, Pennsylvania
JULIE HURST AND ROY BRUBAKER

Blue Rooster Farm is a 94 acre property in south central Pennsylvania, where Julie and Roy have raised grass-fed lamb, beef, and hogs for the past 15 years. The couple's twin daughters were 11-years old at the time of this interview.

Blue Rooster sells their meat through creative partnerships with buying clubs and CSAs. Village Acres in Mifflintown and New Morning Farm near Washington D.C. are two of their well-known partners. About half the meat goes out as retail cuts, and the rest as whole or half animals. The arrangement is that Julie and Roy deliver the meat on CSA pick-up days, but do not need to stay for the whole day.

MOSTLY FAMILY LABOR

Blue Rooster relies on family labor, and has no employees. Julie is home full-time on the farm. Roy works full-time as a District Forester in addition to farming. His job has some flexibility, but is quite demanding of his time.

They extend their labor force from May to Oct by contract

grazing their steers. A professional herdsman takes the cattle to rented land, manages their day-to-day care, and is paid based on weight gain.

TIME MANAGEMENT TIP: PROFESSIONAL ADVICE

2013 was an interesting year for Julie and Roy. They hired a farm-savvy business consultant, Kitchen Table Consultants, to help them streamline their business. They knew they wanted the farm to do more than just pay the taxes and out-of-pocket expenses. They wanted a reasonable return for the amount of time they were putting in. It was time for an unbiased second opinion.

The results were rewarding. Enterprises which were not a good fit for the farm and family were eliminated. Those which did fit and were moving the couple towards their goals were improved. Julie and Roy found the process to be energizing. While fewer in number, their farm enterprises are now more clearly focused. "Our business is better run", says Julie, "and our time is better spent".

YES TO TECHNOLOGY

"Our customer base is very connected", explains Julie. Blue Rooster has an interactive website. Customers can pre-order cuts of meat to be dropped off at a CSA or buying club point. A very useful function is real-time inventory control. Julie and Roy have also found Iphones to be a worthwhile investment for staying connected to their customers.

PLANNING STYLES

With Roy working off the farm, evening is the time when the couple touches base and plans ahead. The upcoming week is discussed over the weekend.

Julie handles most of the administrative tasks on the farm because she is based at home. The framework for a typical day is animal chores morning and evening, with office work in between. Those hours quickly pass with bookkeeping, marketing, organizing butcher dates, customer contact, filling orders, and tracking inventory. Other days are 'driving' days, dedicated to hauling animals or picking up and delivering meat.

Julie writes her daily plans in a notebook, which subsequently serves as a record of completed tasks. The most common interruptions which derail her plans are unexpected visitors and equipment breakdown.

ADVICE FOR NEW FARMERS

"Don't feel bad about having an off-farm job for safety and security", suggests Julie. This can give you the freedom to build your farm as time and money allow.

Be clear about what you really want. Is it the actual farming, or is it the rural lifestyle you desire? You do not have to make a full-time living at farming to have the lifestyle. You can live the rural lifestyle without going all the way into full-time farming for income. However, if you do want farming to be your income as well as your lifestyle, approach it as a business.

"We took too long to hire a bookkeeper", reflects Julie.

"Treating your farm like a business means playing to your strengths and weaknesses. Don't try to do everything yourself", she suggests. "Do what you do well, but find someone else with expertise you lack."

There are many ways to get help besides hiring staff. You can outsource or contract any profession from bookkeeping to fence repair. Creative partnerships and barter are great ways to pair up wants and needs. The resulting synergies will be far better than burning yourself out trying to do everything singlehandedly.

FORKS FARM

Orangeville, Pennsylvania
THE HOPKINS FAMILY

John and Todd Hopkins and their three children have owned this 85-acre property since 1986, starting with the simple goal of putting good food on the table. Today, Forks Farm is a multi-faceted enterprise providing local and sustainable products to a wide range of customers. Two of the children are in college, and the youngest is boarding away for high school. Help comes in the form of interns and volunteers.

Forks Farm raises grass-fed beef, free-range eggs, pastured turkeys, pastured chicken, and woodlot pork. The chickens are processed on the farm. Meat and eggs are sold through several channels. Customers preorder halves or wholes, and a self-service retail space offers frozen cuts of meat and other products such as cheese. Several restaurants feature Forks Farm products on their menu. Farther afield, John and Todd also organize buyers clubs in major cities.

John and Todd are locally famous for the twice-monthly farmers markets they host on their property June through October. They sell not only their own meats, but also invite other sustainable farmers and businesses to sell complimentary products, offering a "one-stop shopping" destination for consumers.

Neither John nor Todd work full-time on the farm. Todd holds a full-time job as a Pediatric Physical Therapist. John runs his own Forestry Consulting business. Both are active in their community. Fortunately, each of their off-farm jobs offers flexible scheduling.

There is one more side-business which takes attention in the warm months. Camping is provided on a river which flows through the farm.

All of these micro-businesses add up to a staggering amount of clerical work and logistics planning in addition to daily animal care.

LABOR SITUATION

As their business grew, Forks Farm's labor force evolved from neighborly volunteers to live-in interns. Nowadays they routinely hire one or two interns during the busy season which starts in spring and continues through the fall. They offer a stipend on top of room and board. "Having a good intern takes care of the day to day chores and frees me up to work on other projects", says John. "It lets me be available on Market Day, and leave the farm when I need to". John and Todd conduct extensive interviews, reference checks, and background screening in choosing their interns.

FACTORS THAT CHANGE THE DAILY PLAN

There is an endless variety of factors that can alter the plan for the day at Forks Farm. Animal emergencies top the list, from escapes to medical issues. Customer interactions also take time, but is the lifeblood of the business. Todd and John set aside one day a week that someone is available to welcome visitors. "Old" customers know the routine in the self-service store, but new or prospective customers are personally shown around.

USE OF TECHNOLOGY

John and Todd have a farm website and subscribe to an email marketing service. In 2010, they made a revolutionary upgrade in technology. The success of the buying clubs combined with a general upswing in business was producing an enormous burden in terms of coallating orders, creating invoices, and physically packaging the orders. Errors and product shortages were unavoidable due to the time lag between orders placed and orders received.

Forks Farm now boasts a real-time, web-based ordering system based on a portable Ipad. The system automatically generates packing lists, invoices, and customer confirmations. Out-of-stock items are instananeously updated and cannot be ordered. The system was an immediate success. It cuts in half the time needed to prepare for buying club deliveries, and eliminates human error.

TIME MANAGEMENT TIP: MASTER CALENDAR

John and Todd can look at their calendar in December and tell you what they will be doing on a set day in August. This level of pre-season planning is critical to their business.

Each enterprise is time-sensitive. Take for example a batch of meat birds destined to be sold at an August 6 Farmers Market. Butchering must be organized for August 5. The chicks must arrive 9 weeks prior, in the first week of June. This requires placing an order with the hatchery in February, before the most desirable dates sell out.

Every one of their projects has a similar timeline. One of John's favorite butchers books a year in advance—forcing an appointment for animals not yet conceived! Picture a juggler spinning ten china plates in the air—you now have a picture of life at Forks Farm. John and Todd manage this aspect of the business with a master calendar which lists every critical task and event for at least 12 months out. This allows them to plan every detail for success, avoid overscheduling, and prevent duplication of effort.

TIME MANAGEMENT TIP: NO NAGGIN'

As a self-described "Type A" personality, Todd bounces out of bed each morning with a clear vision of the day's critical tasks. Because she works off the farm, she must communicate these priorities to John. When the farm was small, she would just mention these thoughts as she headed out the door, or in passing during the day. However, as the farm grew more complex, an unintended consequence developed. Every conversation turned into a follow-up session on projects. "I felt like I was always nagging John," Todd reflects. She came up with a different tactic. She leaves a note in the morning outlining what she sees as important tasks, so John can work them into his plan for the day. Now, the couple's precious face-to-face conversations are more meaningful and less iritating than, "did you finish the...."

ADVICE FOR NEW FARMERS

One of the most important things John and Todd did in the early days of farming was to take a course in Holistic Resource Management (see Appendix). This is a decision-making framework tied to your personal goals, values, and resources. Courses are offered worldwide. They had no idea at that time how successful and complicated their farm business would become. The principles of HRM continue to help them align their daily activities with their long-term goals.

John also encourages new farmers to start small. "Focus on one thing and do it well. Don't try to get too big, too fast". Todd suggests "take a course in livestock handling if you're going to raise animals. You don't have to reinvent the wheel—there are experienced people out there who love to help beginners".

HAMEAU FARM

Belleville, Pennsylvania
AUDREY GAY RODGERS

The Rodgers family has raised prize-winning Ayrshire cattle for three generations, and Gay is carrying on the tradition. The farm boasts 110 acres of grassland. At the time of this writing, there were 26 cows in the milking string and 26 heifers coming along. Gay utilizes sustainable, grass-based production methods. In the summer, the farm transforms into an overnight educational camp for girls ages 8-14. Gay even organizes international trips with her campers. In 2015, for example, she took a group to Scotland to visit the homeland of the Ayrshire breed. Gay is also a firm believer in diversifying her interests beyond the farm. In the fall and winter, she teaches Dale Carnegie courses at the local high school. The young people learn communication skills, strengthen interpersonal skills, and build confidence.

LABOR

Gay has one full-time employee year-round, and an additional part-timer in the fall and winter. Summer camp employs a staff of ten including cooks, residential advisors, instructors, and counselors. A counselor-in-training program grooms exceptional campers for these highly sought-after leadership positions. Farm life is integrated into the camp program. The girls participate in routine chores each morning and evening, using a rotational schedule to focus on a different animal each day. In addition to the dairy cattle and calves, there are sheep, laying hens, goats, and dogs to care for.

ORGANIZING THE DAYS

Gay organizes her daily responsibilities in two categories: non-negotiable and negotiable. The most important daily non-negotiable is milking. Milking machines go on by 6:30 am and 4:30 pm. All other activities revolve around those deadlines. Projects, repairs, and other more flexible activities must make way for milking. Other non-negotiable endeavors vary by season. In winter, for example, Gay attends Camp Fairs to market her programs. Virtually every weekend January through March are taken up with what she refers to as her "second job". And yes, there is a "third job": teaching Dale Carnegie courses to high school students. In between these immoveable obligations in her schedule are bits of time for other projects. "My life is never boring", reflects Gay.

GOOD OLD-FASHIONED NOTEBOOK

Gay does rely on modern technology to interface with the public. Her smart phone is her constant companion, and the farm website and Facebook provide a 24/7 online presence. However, she and her full-time employee find that nothing beats a good old-fashioned notebook for day-to-day communication in the barn. Onto that paper go the critical details that make a dairy barn run smoothly: who is coming into heat, whose milk looks a bit flaky, which calf needs some extra TLC, what visitors or suppliers are stopping by, etc.

SEASONAL CHANGES

Gay does not really have a slow season, but her routine and responsibilities do change with the season as does the people she spends time with. Fall semester finds her interacting with bright teenagers, and finding satisfaction in building their self-esteem. In the winter, Gay is face-to-face with enthusiastic prospective campers and their families from all walks of life. Spring brings her attention 100% back to the farm in the season of renewal, and summer is camp time. This diversified schedule keeps her fresh and enthusiastic throughout the year.

ADVICE FOR NEW FARMERS

Not surprisingly, Gay is an advocate of diversity in life. "No matter how much you love farming", she suggests, "you will be a better farmer if you get away from it periodically." She is a big fan of joining breed organizations. This type of networking brings benefits both socially and professionally.

Also important is to schedule personal time for you and your family. Pencil it right into your calendar, rather than waiting for "time to open up".

Plan frequent changes in your routine. No matter how

much you start out loving it, the same routine will eventually lead to dissatisfaction. People thrive on change, novelty, and adventure. It's your farm, your business, and your life: you can make it as interesting as you wish.

HERRING'S GREEN GRASS FARM

Schuylkill Haven, Pennsylvania
WAYNE HERRING

2014 was a pivotal year for Wayne and Katherine Herring and their four children ages 3-11. Wayne had been farming for five years while working full time. Starting with rented land, he had purchased 21 acres of land and built a house while developing a grass-based, direct-marketed farm enterprise. In 2014 he left his corporate job to dedicate his time to the farm and developing a consulting business. That year he raised 1500 chickens, 40 hogs, 13 goats, 80 turkeys, and 120 laying hens.

Consumer-direct sales are the business model for Herring's Green Grass Farm. All products are sold directly to consumers who pre-order and come out to the farm. There are also several restaurant clients.

LABOR

Wayne and his family handle most of the work on the farm. His cousin helps a few hours a week and on chicken processing days. There is also a group of friends who volunteer on a regular basis.

Wayne handles the daily chores and projects. His main areas of responsibility are managing the hogs and chickens, customer contact, marketing and promotion, accounting, livestock transportation, feed purchasing, organizing butcher instructions, and the never-ending repair and maintenance.

MORNING PLANS AND PAPER CALENDARS

Wayne begins each day before the sun rises with a planning session. He reviews yesterday's To Do list and the upcoming day's activities. These feed into two lists: "Things That Must Be Done Today", and "Things It Would Be Nice To Do Today". He then prioritizes each list in order of importance.

Although modern technology does play a role in Wayne's business, online calendars do not. He finds a paper calendar much more effective. He blocks out time with highlighters, using color codes. Blue, for example, signifies family time. This tangible calendar works much better for him than online versions.

SOCIAL MEDIA UTILIZATION

As a direct marketer, customer relations are critical to Wayne's business. He uses technology to communicate with customers and promote his products. He carries a smartphone, maintains a farm website, and uses Facebook and a farm blog to maintain an ongoing conversation with his customer base.

ADMINISTRATIVE TIME

Wayne carves out office time in the middle of each day to handle the purely administrative tasks such as paying bills and responding to emails. He and his wife share the burden of accounting input and analysis using Quicken.

SUDDEN CHANGES OF PLAN

No matter how organized the day starts out, sudden detours do take place. Customer phone calls are top priority for Wayne, demanding his full attention. New customers occasionally drop in to see the farm for themselves, and Wayne gives them an in-depth tour. Sick animals or mechanical problems with essential systems like water constitute a 'drop everything' emergency. Although he tries to keep his two businesses separate, inevitably he sometimes needs to attend a meeting or conference call on short notice.

SEASONALITY

The Herrings have structured their farm so they can have downtime in the winter. The only animals they keep year-round are the laying hens. This allows Wayne to allocate more time in the winter to his consulting business. All year round, Sundays are protected as a family day

FORMAL TIME MANAGEMENT TRAINING

Planning and analysis come naturally to Wayne because of the many years he spent in the business world. Most of his positions were as an individual contributor, aligning his priorities and tasks with overall goals. For 9 years he had the privilege of working with a business coach who had a professional interest in time management. One of his most memorable assignments was to periodically challenge Wayne to create a "Not To Do" list, as opposed to the traditional "To Do" list.

Wayne reflects that although the planning process appears the same in business as in farming, it is the underlying sense of urgency which sets the two apart. An unfinished task in the office may interrupt the workflow, but does not normally result in death. On the farm, untended issues with health, feed, or water could have disastrous results

ADVICE FOR NEW FARMERS

"It's not just a job—it's your life" summarizes Wayne. If you go into farming thinking it can be a 9-5 job and then you go home, you need to rethink your expectations. You will of course try to create a work/life balance, but things will come up that need to be handled in a timely manner. No matter how good an operation you run, there will be emergencies such as escaped animals, illness, mechanical breakdowns, extreme weather, the list goes on. You will have to be prepared to deal with the unplanned "wild cards".

Wayne also suggests having your eyes wide open regarding the financial realities. If you want to farm as a full-time occupation, you will have thousands of dollars invested. Think carefully about the difference between farming part-time and full-time in terms of financial outlay.

Wayne also brings the discussion back to the topic of time

management: don't scoff at the concept or assume it's only important in an office setting. You will accomplish a lot more and be more successful in farming if you plan ahead and stay focused. Don't fly by the seat of your pants just because you don't have a boss setting your priorities.

JUJO ACRES

Loysville, Pennsylvania
JONAS AND JUDY STOLTZFUS

Jonas and Judy raise certified organic grass-fed beef, and have the distinction of being one of the few third party certified beef herds in Central Pennsylvania. They purchased their 73 acre farm in 1971 and have been free from herbicides, chemical fertilizers, and pesticides since 1980. In 1999, they obtained organic certification through Pennsylvania Certified Organic and USDA. They also participate in certification programs from Animal Welfare Approved® and American Grassfed®.

The cattle are a blend of Limousin, Charolais, and Angus genetics. The current herd numbers 55 beef cattle from a base herd of 18 brood cows. Rotational grazing is the cornerstone of the operation. All the beef is sold direct to consumers as quarters and halves. Many customers come to the farm, and Jonas also delivers to drop-off points in nearby Harrisburg and Carlisle.

LABOR

Judy and Jonas are in their 70's and run the farm without full-time help. Subsequently, they are exceptionally well-versed in the art of getting things done efficiently while knowing when to ask for help. At the time of this writing, the couple was in the process of transitioning the farm to the next generation.

The division of labor has adapted over the years, as the couple raised their 4 children. For 12 years, Judy taught her children at home and during this time managed a small goat herd. She made cheese, butter and yogurt, integrating these products with her garden produce to provide nourishing, organic food for her family. She now handles the administration, accounting, and office support. Jonas takes care of the livestock from birth through butchering, as well as the grazing management and infrastructure.

ORGANIZING THE DAYS

Jonas uses the classic To Do List to organize his days and weeks. He crafts a new list each week, adjusting it daily to reflect completed tasks, shifting priorities, and unforeseen circumstances. He starts each morning with quiet reading and reflection. This provides the ideal setting to plan his days. Beyond routine chores, there is a limited amount of discretionary daylight hours available. Jonas follows two unifying principles in prioritizing his activities: 1) what are his goals and do these tasks support them and 2) what is the most efficient way to approach these tasks?

ADVICE TO NEW FARMERS

Jonas notes that prioritizing will be the most important and yet the most difficult aspect of farming. You will be surrounded by tasks of all sizes screaming for attention. But if you allow yourself to step back and visualize the steps needed to reach your goals, your efforts will ultimately pay off.

Very importantly, Jonas also cautions that, "some things will not happen unless you get help". It can be admittedly difficult to pay someone if money is tight, but you simply cannot do everything yourself. Know when to reach out for another pair of hands or skill set, or important things may stay at the bottom of the list for way too long. Like, forever.

Build time into your life for planning and reflection. Ensure that your hard work is moving you towards your goals. It's all too easy to lose sight of the big picture when you are perpetually busy and distracted.

Jonas speaks from experience when he reflects on goal-setting. He grew up on a farm, but he and Judy did not get into farming together until their late 20's, when they bought JuJo Acres as a place to raise their children. They steadily built the business using the principles discussed above.

CLOSING THOUGHTS

When not working cattle or moving fence, Jonas enjoys writing poetry. He shares one his favorites about life at JuJo Acres:

THE WHY

"Ya concentrate most on the why", Alex says, "the how comes along as ya go".
Rememberin' the reason for all that I do
The how's a small part of the show.
So why do I get up so early each morn
Quite oft long before the day's ea'n born
'n think of the cow's , chickens ,ole horse, 'n goats
Got my pot 'o coffee, bowl o' raisins, milk, honey 'n oats
Then move round the farm, at a slow steady pace
Takin' care o' those animals, this isn't a race
'n occasionally think of the why, I'm doing this stuff at our farm.
It's cause of the person who once told me ,
"Jonas, you saved my life", now that's a real solid bonus.
Another one said, "You saved my Dad's life", and I asked him, how?
"From the bone broth of an ole grassfed organic cow
and the recipe how to make more".
So these are the " whys" that get me on the move
An' keep this ole man in the organic groove
Of doin' what I do for me 'n my friends ' health
It sure as heaven ain't just for my own personal wealth.

Takin' care of the land and the animals too
Gives me a reason for livin' I'm just tellin' you.

Jonas K. Stoltzfus,
5:00AM Saturday, August 3, 2013

LE-ARA FARMS

Wothington, Pennsylvania
LARA AND DOUG SHIELDS

Lara and Doug run a thriving raw milk business spanning several hundred acres on three farms. The home property has been in the family since 1894, making Lara the 7th generation. Between the milking string and replacements, there are over 300 head of Holsteins. The Shields grow their own corn and forage. Raw milk is their centerpiece enterprise, bringing customers to the farm six days a week to fill their own bottles under the terms of the Pennsylvania raw milk license.

FAMILY LABOR ONLY

Le-Ara has no employees. Lara and Doug have clearly delineated responsibilities. Lara is in charge of the cows. Doug handles all the field work. Although the workload is heavy and the hours long, the boundaries are clear. When a problem arises, no time is wasted deciding who should respond. A sick cow prompts a call to Lara, while a broken piece of equipment gets Doug's full attention.

Meals are taken in the evening after the day's work is done.

Lara specializes in long-cooking dishes that can be started in the morning and eaten anytime later.

DIVIDE AND CONQUER PAPERWORK

There is an enormous amount of paperwork involved in this type of operation. Lara handles the clerical end of things, and is transitioning from a paper-based system to more of a computerized one. No matter what the system is, many hours are necessary to stay on top of paying bills, keeping track of cattle registration, breeding records, herd health, classification programs, and interfacing with regulatory officials regarding the raw milk business.

FORWARD-PLANNING SAVES TIME

Emergencies in Lara's cow herd are rare. Her operating philosophy is to prevent problems by planning ahead and being proactive in herd health. She is with her cows every day, observing every detail of behavior and attitude. She also believes strongly in the team approach, rather than trying to do everything herself. Her team includes an expert nutritionist and a outstanding veterinary clinic. They work together to stay ahead of the curve on health and nutrition, working proactively, not reactively. Lara does not take shortcuts when it comes to herd health. She has observed that today's shortcut often leads to tomorrow's "crash and burn". From a time-saving standpoint, this way of doing things saves days lost to crisis management.

TYPICAL DAY

It is a testimony to Lara's organization skills that she can describe a typical day. Morning milking and related chores start at 6:00, with breakfast around 8:00. Raw milk customers can come between 7:00 and 9:00 am to have Lara fill their bottles. Evening milking starts at 5:15 with raw milk sales between 6:00 and 7:00 pm. In between milking are precious, flexible hours available for other cow work and projects.

ADVICE FOR NEW FARMERS

Lara's raw milk business is thriving, she enjoys a close-knit family, and she bounces out of bed every morning looking forward to the day. However, she cautions new farmers to think long and hard before choosing dairy farming as an occupation. "It is very expensive to set up", she says. "You will work 14 hour days (or longer in case of a crisis), and 90 hour weeks—and you'll still be short on cash. You can outsource some aspects of the farm, but your herd will suffer if you personally are not working with them and observing them on a daily basis". For those determined to milk cows, Lara encourages them to seek niche markets like raw milk, rather than build their entire business plan on bulk sales to a milk cooperative.

MYSTIC SPRINGS FARM

Richfield, Pennsylvania
GILES AND MARCIA WICKHAM

Mystic Springs is a small-scale biologically sustainable farm offering CSA memberships to the public and specialty produce for restaurants and health food stores. Giles and Marcia bought this seven-acre property in 2010, after operating their CSA on rented ground for three years. They grow vegetables year-round using a combination of traditional row gardens, raised beds, hoophouses, and a large greenhouse. The vegetables are harvested weekly and brought to a local farmers' market for pick-up. Fresh eggs and a fall harvest of chestnuts from the stately trees gracing their land round out their product line.

The farm is just one aspect of a very busy life.

The couple has four children ranging in age from twenty-four to three. two of whom are homeschooled. The farmhouse, though charming and cozy, will be undergoing age-related remodeling for the foreseeable future. Giles works full-time off the farm as head chef in a nearby public school system, tapping into his previous career in the restaurant field. He is the ideal candidate for this position, understanding the supply chain from producer to plate. From a personal standpoint, the job is a good fit because it offers flexible scheduling and time off in the summer. This enables Giles to be on the farm when most needed.

Giles and Marcia's farming methods utilize hand-labor and small, self-propelled equipment rather than tractor power. Because their low-lying soils are high in clay and often wet, soil compaction would be a risk with heavy equipment. However, these farming methods do increase the amount of hand labor performed by the family.

LABOR SITUATION

Giles and Marcia do most of the work on the farm, with help from their children and occasional interns and volunteers. They have had very positive experiences with college-age students, and will lean in that direction should they decide to bring in help in a more formal or permanent way.

TIME MANAGEMENT TIP: DIVIDE AND CONQUER

The house and farm work are loosely divided into two domains. Marcia keeps the household and children's education running smoothly, while Giles organizes and prioritizes the farm work. Having a designated individual overseeing each area prevents redundancy or it's polar opposite, neglect. "I thought *you* were watering the seedlings", is the farmer's version of "I thought *you* were picking Johnny up from soccer".

Marcia and Giles tend to work off separate lists, collaborating on an on-going roster of long-term projects to be tackled as time and finances permit. "I keep a running list", quips Giles, "and if I cross off five things, I usually add ten". An important part of the daily routine is to check in with each other as to who needs help with "two-man" jobs and when each spouse will be available.

Giles sets his priorities around the CSA. Any task directly impacting the harvest gets top priority. These customers have entrusted Mystic Springs with capital and high expectations. In the true nature of community supported agriculture, Giles and Marcia act in partnership with their CSA members.

FACTORS THAT CHANGE THE DAILY PLAN

Family comes first no matter what the daily plan dictates. There are days when the younger kids just need the undivided attention of mom and/or dad. Work stops, or shifts to child-friendly, side-by-side tasks. Sometimes the whole family drops everything and jumps in the car for a field trip. As Giles puts it, "at the end of our lives, that's going to be more important than whether the onions got weeded".

But the onions and seventy-nine other vegetables are also important, too. The discovery of plants in distress is cause for immediate action. A disaster in the making such as transplants needing water or a crop overtaken by weeds must be taken care of immediately, or the CSA might suffer a shortfall at harvest time. Thus, the daily work remains consistent with the long-term goal of supporting the CSA.

USE OF TECHNOLOGY

The couple uses cell phones, and maintains a website for the CSA. Member communications are via email or phone. Future plans include online payment capabilities for subscriptions.

ADVICE FOR NEW FARMERS

Plans and dreams can be a double-edged sword: motivating but overwhelming. Giles and Marcia have ambitions ranging from fruit trees to hydroelectric power. "We have plans that will take us until we're ninety years old to accomplish", explains Giles, "but if we think too hard about how far we have to go, it drives us nuts". He suggests getting in the habit of regularly taking stock of how far you have come with your farm and what you have accomplished.

Giles also has a strong belief in young people trying their hand at farming if they think it is what they want to do with their life. He offers an "out-of-the-box" suggestion. "If you are passionate about farming, don't go to college right out of high school. Find work on every farm you can that does the type of farming you want to do. Learn from experienced people who are successful. If you change your mind about farming, move on to a new career choice and college if needed".

NEW MORNING FARM

HUSTONTOWN, Pennsylvania
JIM AND MOIE CRAWFORD

New Morning Farm covers 95 acres in South Central Pennsylvania, where Jim and Moie Crawford have grown organic vegetables since 1976. They produce over 60 different vegetables, fruits, and herbs in a year-round production system utilizing a heated greenhouse and two high tunnels. They sell retail at four weekly farmers markets and also have wholesale customers. The Crawfords are founding members of the Tuscarora Growers Cooperative, which coordinates organic farms and growers in central PA to serve restaurants, groceries and markets in the PA-DC region. They have two children, now grown and following non-farm career paths.

LABOR

New Morning Farm employs 25 seasonal workers, 12 of whom are apprentices with managerial and decision-making roles. 6-8 employees work year round. Jim and Moie take great pains to attract and retain their employees. Salaries are competitive and include bonuses and incentives tied to the farm's performance. Room and board are provided. Jobs are carefully structured so employees have both responsibility and authority. A team approach is the prevailing culture.

EVOLUTION IN SCALE

New Morning Farm was not always big. "We started small, and we grew to our current size", reflects Jim, "and we _much_ prefer this size. Our farm is now able to operate in a calm and professional manner".

Adequate staffing and time management are subjects that Jim has been particularly interested in throughout his farm's 40+ years of growth. When New Morning was small and had no employees, the workload was overwhelming and the stress unrelenting. Money was always tight. Small luxuries and vacations were difficult to afford. The farm was dominating the family's life, but not providing a comfortable middle-class income.

Jim could see this pattern playing out in many of the small farms he knew. He came to think of it as a puzzle to be solved. The idealized vision of a sustainable farm was a small, family-owned operation. However, sustainability encompassed much more than farming practices. A sustainable farm had to be profitable enough to meet the family's financial goals, yet require a reasonable workload which would not lead to burnout and bitterness. There had to be a critical size and scale for each farm which optimized those goals. In today's economy, that critical size is often larger than in year's past.

Jim and Moie took steps to improve the situation at New Morning Farm in the 1990s when they hired their first apprentices. As they embraced their new roles as employers, and developed the team approach which would characterize their farm, the overwork and stress began to ease up. As the saying goes, they never looked back. The team of skilled employees is now an integral part of New Morning Farm. Everyone, including Jim and Moie, works reasonable hours and has time for other interests.

CREW MEETING STARTS THE DAY

Teamwork is more than just a buzzword at New Morning Farm. It defines how the business operates. Each morning begins with a meeting where the staff reviews the written plan for the day. The tasks are clearly listed and names are assigned. That way, everyone knows not only what he is in charge of, but what his teammates are doing. "Every person has a job, and every job has a person", explains Jim. It is the crew leaders' responsibility to ensure that the daily plan dovetails with the annual master plan for the farm.

TECHNOLOGY

The day to day work has not become overly dependent on modern technology because the farm does not have cell phone reception. The staff uses walkie-talkies to communicate over distances. The farm does maintain an informative website of interest to both job seekers and customers.

ADVICE FOR NEW FARMERS

"You can't do everything yourself on a diversified farm, and keep your sanity", quips Jim. He strongly believes that if someone is planning on farming full-time, their vision should include competent help. The very nature of a diversified farm means multiple enterprises that need close attention. You don't have to think of it as "grunt" labor, he adds. The team approach works wonders for bringing out the best in people.

Finding the help you need and figuring out the right size and scale for your operation are two important keys to truly sustainable farming.

ONE STRAW FARM

White Hall, Maryland
DREW AND JOAN NORMAN

One Straw Farm is a family owned and operated farm in northern Baltimore County, Maryland. On seventy-five acres near the Maryland/Pennsylvania state line, Joan and Drew Norman produce vegetables for 1800 members, sell to five restaurants, and attend five farmers markets. Joan describes the couple's division of labor in simple terms: *"Drew grows it, and I sell it".* The farm began thirty-three years ago as a wholesale operation on three rented acres, and grew from there. When Joan and Drew offered their first CSA shares to eight customers in the 1990's, they unleashed a tidal wave of consumer demand in the city and surrounds of Baltimore. The CSA expanded steadily until they were both able to trade their off-farm careers for full-time farming.

LABOR STRATEGY

One Straw's success is founded on hiring talented people and keeping them happy. They have twenty full-time employees, ten being H2A workers. In charge of their daily work is

Miguel, in the essential role of full-time crew manager.

The crew is responsible for picking, packing, cultivating, weeding, and other tasks which bring the harvest to the customer. The overriding philosophy at One Straw is to enable each employee to discover and specialize in the task they do best. Each worker naturally tends to gravitate to a specific kind of work. *"It becomes a source of pride",* observes Joan, *"to be the best tomato picker, the fastest bean picker, the tidiest buncher, etc."* Joan's greenhouse is a shining example of this. At one point, Joan was having trouble keeping up with that end of the operation. She offered the responsibility to Miquel's wife Carmela, who was thrilled with the opportunity. *"She does a much better job with the greenhouse than I ever did"*, says Joan. Carmela does a superb job of caring for the plants and keeping things organized. So Joan steps out of the way, lets her do her job without interference, and everyone is happy.

CSA members are entitled to eight types of produce each week. They can box their own shares from bulk bins at the farm or a farmers markets, or get their shares prepacked at one of the forty-five delivery drop points.

It is a mind-boggling weekly achievement to organize the produce into pre-packed shares, farmers market selections, on-farm pick-up bins, and restaurant orders. The packing shed serves as the communications headquarters. A dry erase board lists the tasks associated with each objective. Miguel keeps the team's efforts coordinated and on target.

TECHNOLOGY

One Straw maintains a website filled with practical information on their products and services. They accept online payments for CSA shares.

SEASONALITY

One Straw Farm CSA shares begin in June and end at Thanksgiving. Joan and Drew do not grow winter shares. They value the downtime in December for repairs and maintenance, financial analysis, and forward planning. The lull is short, however, as CSA sign-ups resume in January.

PAPERWORK

Joan handles the administrative end of the business. She spends three to four hours every day on clerical tasks such as email, bills, banking, payroll, and research. She does not designate specific office hours, but grabs the time on an as-available basis.

OUTSOURCING

Joan no longer believes in the Supermom myth. She hires a part-time person to do laundry five hours a week, and a cleaning lady every other week. This frees her to do other projects and not feel overwhelmed by the general state of the house. Her only regret is that she didn't do it sooner, when her now-grown children were smaller. *"I debated whether or not to hire help in the house,"* Joan recollects, *"but when I did it was like a big, black cloud lifted off our shoulders. We have a very happy household now. Let's face it, there are only 2 things no one else can do for you: love your kids, and sleep with your husband"*.

ADVICE FOR NEW FARMERS

Joan reminds aspiring farmers that every farm is unique. Observe as many farms as you can to gather ideas and knowledge, but don't expect to find a single magic formula for success. As you move forward with your farm, you will find your own rhythm and lifestyle which fits your personality. *"Farming is not for the faint of heart,"* summarizes Joan. *"It is a lifestyle—a calling—not just a job. You have to figure out what crop or livestock fits your system, and how best to sell it".*

As for day-to-day survival, Drew's advice is simple. *"Start with the biggest fire, and put it out".*

OVER THE MOON FARM

Rebersburg, Pennsylvania
LYN GARLING AND PATTY NEINER

Over The Moon Farm is a twenty-six-acre certified organic, grass-based operation. Lyn and Patty sell hay, custom raise dairy heifers, and raise meat for direct sale to consumers. Their main products are chicken, pork, and turkey. They typically raise 1000 broilers in six batches from May-October plus one batch of Thanksgiving turkeys. The pork comes from two-three batches of eight to ten piglets per year.

Over The Moon sells their meat through weekly farmers markets, and in partnership with local CSA pick-up days on a preorder basis.

LABOR

The biggest time management challenge for Lyn and Patty is that they both work full-time off the farm. Their jobs also require frequent travel. Both are fortunate, however, that their positions allow for flexible hours. This enables them to accomplish time-sensitive farmwork. Although they do not have employees per se, they do have neighbors willing to work part-time as needed.

PAPERWORK UNDER COVER OF DARKNESS

Lyn handles the majority of the administrative and customer service end of the operation. With daylight being so precious, she tackles these tasks early in the morning or after dark.

WEEKLY PLAN

Every weekend, Lyn and Patty sit down to plan the upcoming week. The essential discussion points are, "what task(s) needs to be done", "who is available to perform these tasks", and "who is traveling this week?" Lyn creates a Master List divided into 4 Quadrants. (Note: daily chores do not appear on this list).

1. Things that must happen for the farm(example: arrange hauling for market hogs with a fixed slaughter date).
2. Things that must happen for Lyn or Patty's job (example: projects to complete while working undisturbed from home).
3. Household Management and Personal Care (examples: inspect cars, shop for groceries, dentist appointment).
4. Miscellaneous/Don't Forget! (example: find hired help for a market day).

Based on this input, Lyn ends up with a 3-dimensional "road map" that takes in to account time, physical space, and daylight. "It's a challenging type of planning", says Lyn, "because a farm is a physical entity with biological needs".

The completed plan ends up on a clipboard which Lyn carries with her and annotates as the day/week unfolds. She copies items off of Quadrant 1 as a stand-alone list if needed for farm helpers.

WEATHER REPORT BEGINS THE DAY

Checking the weather and email starts off the morning at Over The Moon Farm. Both may result in adjustments to the weekly plan. The weather obviously affects farm activities. The email often brings work-related mandates that must be worked into the schedule.

VISITS AND FARM TOURS

One thing Lyn and Patty do not have much time for are visits, chats, and farm tours. Although they are happy to arrange something with other farmers, they do not offer "farm tours" as a service. Over the Moon Farm does participate in the yearly PASA farm tour in August. In general, they value their time at home either for productive tasks or much-needed personal time.

TIME MANAGEMENT TRAINING

At various times in her professional life, Lyn has taken seminars and classes in time management in a corporate setting. Although most of the information was not directly applicable to farming, one concept rings true: "first things first". Lyn finds she must fight the urge to do the easy or fun things first. Those might not be the most important relative to her long-term goals. This is where the weekly plan helps her stay on track.

ADVICE FOR NEW FARMERS

Focus on your keystone enterprise first and add on others as the market asks for it and that fit into your management plan relatively easily. Try to focus on the things you can do well and like to do. Be realistic in terms of the time requirements, the income potential, and the risk associated with each project. Don't get stuck on a pet project if there's no market for it. Be flexible and allow yourself to drop something.

No matter what your personal views on wealth may be, if your farm is a business, money and time are what makes all things possible. Lyn thinks of money as an energy flow. Her energy flows out through her labor and investment in, say, raising chickens. The energy flows back to her in the form of her customers' appreciation and payment. She doesn't consider *using* money as greedy or evil. As long as it is flowing (not being hoarded just to have it), money is simply another resource that can benefit your farm, family and community. Having said that, she does caution that it is all too easy to get in debt over your head.

In order to handle the business end of your farm wisely, invest in enterprises and infrastructure that have the potential to return money to you on variable timelines (short, middle, long) so you can balance cash flow. Keep track of your expenses relative to income and don't buy stuff you don't need.

Try not to get blind-sided by big bills coming due. Lyn sets aside cash from each market deposit in a savings account for the yearly/monthly payments that are non-negotiable; local taxes, loan payments and insurance.

OWENS FARM

Sunbury Pennsylvania
CAROLINE AND DAVID OWENS

Owens Farm is a 112-acre property in central Pennsylvania, owned by David and Caroline Owens. The land is excellent for raising livestock, having 80 acres in open fields and 40 in woods. David and Caroline run multiple enterprises on the farm. The core business is raising and direct-marketing grass-fed meat. They have Coopworth and Katahdin sheep, Tamworth pigs, and pastured chickens. The flock is currently 100 ewes producing around 200 lambs, which sell either as custom-cut freezer meat or as feeder lambs. They raise their own piglets from farrow to finish, maintaining around six sows year-round. About 600 cornish-cross chickens are started as day-old chicks. and sold through summer and fall. David is also an avid beekeeper, and produces both honey and nucs.

Educational programs are layered on top of the basic livestock operation. Sheep Camp is a weeklong summer program for children. Adopt-A-Sheep is a yearlong, multi-faceted program capturing every aspect of shepherding from birth through yarn. Lambing-Time Slumber Parties bring adventurous groups to the farm during "that wonderful time of year when the lambs are coming left and right". Guided Farm Tours are offered from Spring to Fall. Owens Farm also offers overnight lodging. "The Loft" is a remodelled barn featuring sleeping quarters, private kitchen, and bath.

David and Caroline do not currently have employees. Two of their three children have "grown and flown" since moving to the farm. Their youngest is in high school.

THE ONE THING RULE

It was out of sheer desperation that David and Caroline devised the One Thing Rule in their first summer on the farm. Arriving in July, they were immediately swamped with a broken-down old farmhouse to prep for winter, livestock to acquire, farm buildings to repair, three kids to settle into new schools, and a fledgling business to start from ground zero. They were overwhelmingly busy, yet ended each day feeling unproductive and overwhelmed. What if, they thought, we chose a single task to complete each day instead of disconnected bits and pieces of too many things. This would be the priority during the discretionary time not mandated by chores and other obligations.

At first blush, the concept seemed ridiculous. With so much to do, how could they limit themselves to one? But within the first week, they saw the pay-off. Instead of fifty-two fragments, seven tasks had been completed. A tractor repaired, a fenceline cleared, a shed dejunked, a project handed off to a welder: step by step, things were happening. Large tasks were broken into small ones that could actually be completed. The One Thing became a tool to focus their daily efforts.

"So, what's your one thing today" is still part of the morning ritual. Sometimes the answer is immediate and obvious. Other times, it takes some reflection to sort through the possibilities and decide which is the greater priority. Sometimes the One Thing is a team effort. Other days find David and Caroline going in separate directions.

MONTHLY PLANNING SESSION

The biggest time management challenge on this diversified farm is keeping track of all the details that spell the difference between success and failure. At any one time, there are over twenty enterprises underway, creating a complex matrix of essential tasks and critical deadlines. Caroline keeps things under control with a detailed planning session once a month. Her approach starts with a written timeline for each product and project. Some are fairly simple. The chicken plan, for example, steps quickly from "order chicks" to "set butcher appointments" and "announce pre-orders". Others are much more complex. Running Sheep Camp entails registration, promotion, logistics, personnel, supplies, lesson planning, and timely communication. The Adopt-A-Sheep program runs off a year-long calendar of synchronized activities and communications. Farm repairs and improvements are also part of the monthly review. David and Caroline use this opportunity to debate which projects and ideas should be acted upon in the next 30 days

The key concept is that, no matter how complicated an enterprise may be, every single one can be distilled into discrete tasks to be executed at a specific time. And that is the outcome of the planning session: every task is written in someone's daily planner. When Caroline opens her calendar for the day, the To Do list is already started. The entries may seem random, but she knows that each ties neatly into the big picture, like this example from a late January entry:

- Announce Sheep Camp registrations
- Write Adopt-A-Sheep letter, Pregnant Pause
- Tally up sold pigs..email?
- Order lambing supplies
- Start repairing sow huts
- Send press release for Lambing Slumber Party

For Caroline, this strategy works by capitalizing on a frame of mind that is hard to achieve. Planning future activities, connecting the dots, including the small details that spell success—that is a very specific mindset. It occurs when she is relaxed, unhurried, feeling positive, and unlikely to be disturbed: preferably before the sun rises. Once a month she can make that happen. Then it's off to the races again with "real life": farm work and housekeeping and reacting to real-time events. In her own words, Caroline reflects that "on a typical day when I'm moving fence, feeding animals, working sheep, returning phone calls, trying to get a meal on the table, etc., the farthest thing from my mind is, "Hark! I need to order ribbons for Sheep Camp!" or "if I don't order selenium now, I won't have it 6 weeks before lambing begins". I have to plan it once, write it down, and just get it done without second-guessing myself".

PAPERWORK BEFORE DAWN

There is an enormous amount of clerical work and customer communications supporting this farm. Dave and Caroline are both up before dawn to put in office time before the day gets going. They both carry smart phones to field phone calls and scan email during the day, but as Caroline puts it, "I never have a coherent thought after 8:00 pm".

ADVICE FOR NEW FARMERS

"Make sure you have enough capital and are realistic with your budgeting", cautions Dave. "It will take more money than you think to sustain your farm until it starts generating income".

"Zig when everyone else zags", suggests Caroline. "Let your farm reflect your personality and strengths, and don't feel you have to fit into some pre-made 'farmer' mold. That is the beauty of farming: every single operation is different because of the land and its people. It's your farm—do what works for you".

PAINTED HAND FARM

Sandra Kay Miller
NEWBURG, PENNSYLVANIA

A close look at Painted Hand Farm begs the question, "how does she do it all"? Sandra raises grass-fed beef, humanely-raised rose veal, naturally-browsed goat and pastured fowl for both meat & eggs on her twenty-acre farm in Cumberland County, Pennsylvania. She sells at five Farmers Markets, two of which occur on the same day. She offers a Meat CSA, supplies several buyers clubs, and provides live lambs and goats directly to the ethnic market. Every December, she sells Christmas trees. As the sole proprietor of this complex enterprise, Sandra wears many hats. Her responsibilities include but are not limited to day-to-day animal husbandry, butchering logistics, pricing, accounting, inventory control, marketing, repairs and maintenance, customer relations, regulatory compliance, and staffing. In her 'spare' time, she is a free-lance writer.

LABOR STRATEGY

Sandra hires employees on an as-needed, hourly wage basis. She has a network of people with varying levels of interest and availability. One longtime employee is fully responsible for one of the Sunday Farmers Markets, freeing Sandra up to attend the simultaneous one. Some employees help on a regular basis, while others are called in for special projects. There are even some meat customers who pitch in once in a while.

USE OF TECHNOLOGY

Sandra simplifies her life by using a single smartphone and no landline. Having one phone to answer and one message machine to keep up with does make a difference. She maintain a farm website with online ordering, keeps a blog about farm life, and uses both Facebook and Twitter. Her smartphone doubles as a credit card reader for Farmers Markets. Sandra enjoys solving problems with cutting edge applications, having worked in high tech in her previous career.

TIME MANAGEMENT TIP: PHYSICAL LAYOUT

From the day they bought the farm, Sandra and her husband faced the possibility that she would someday farm alone due to his severe health problems. Accordingly, they designed the infrastructure to minimize the need for dogs or humans to perform routine livestock tasks.

Fenced lanes run in between the pastures, with strategically placed gates the exact width of the lane. Rotating pastures is as simple as opening a gate and letting the animals mosey down the lane. Two gates swung across the lane creates a catch pen. Sandra can worm, trim feet, or catch individual animals without bringing the whole herd into a central handing system as is seen on many farms. To haul livestock, she backs her trailer into the end of the alleyway. The chosen animals are sorted out of the catch pen, quietly shooed down the lane, and backfenced into a tiny corral with the only exit being the trailer door. No rodeos. No stress. No extra help needed.

TIME MANAGEMENT TIP: VOLUNTEER CAREFULLY

Sandra has had periods in her life when she was very active in agriculture-related and community organizations. She stepped back from these time-consuming activities, however, when the operation of the farm came to rest solely on her shoulders. Her physical presence and mental focus were needed at home. Upon reflection, she realized how easily volunteer assignments can multiply and get out of hand. She is now extremely selective about activities which take time away from the farm, and only chooses those which result in tangible benefits to her core business.

TIME MANAGEMENT TIP: JOURNAL-STYLE TO-DO LIST

Despite her comfort with technology, one of Sandra's most important time management tools involves paper and pencil. She keeps her To Do Lists in a bound journal which never leaves the house. "No batteries to run down, and never gets lost," says the self-described techno-geek with a smile. The journal simultaneously functions as a permanent record of tasks accomplished, a storehouse of great ideas, and the daily smorgasborg of things to do. Anyone who has ever experienced a lost, laundered, or rain-soaked-beyond-recognition To Do List can appreciate this method.

ADVICE FOR NEW FARMERS

"When you begin", suggests Sandra, "you need to focus 100% on your business. Don't divide your attention between too many unrelated activities."

"And it's ok not to offer every possible product or service", she adds. "If something is not working for you, don't be afraid to discontinue it. You can't afford too many non-productive uses of your time". Sandra has followed her own advice over the years. She no longer sells purebred goats for breeding stock or guardian dog puppies. These were two fledgling enterprises that turned out to be more trouble than they were worth. The product lines she continues year in and year out are those that are win-wins for all involved: the customers, the farm business, and Sandra Kay Miller herself.

POLYFACE FARM Inc.

Swoope, Virginia
JOEL SALATIN

Polyface Farm is a multi-generational, pasture-based family farm direct-marketing salad-bar beef, pigerator pork, pastured poultry, and forest products to more than 6000 families plus retail outlets, restaurants, and metropolitan buying clubs. It was in 1982 that Joel Salatin returned full-time to his family farm to resume and refine his parents' unconventional farming methods. Joel's willingness to share his knowledge and ideals fueled the fledgling sustainable farming movement, bringing celebrity status to the family. Polyface has been featured in SMITHSONIAN MAGAZINE, NATIONAL GEOGRAPHIC, GOURMET and countless other radio, television and print media. Profiled on the Lives of the 21st Century series with Peter Jennings on ABC World News, his after-broadcast chat room fielded more hits than any other segment to date. It achieved iconic status as the grass farm featured in the NEW YORK TIMES bestseller OMNIVORE'S DILEMMA by food writer guru Michael Pollan.

THE FACES BEHIND POLYFACE

Polyface Farm currently supports four generations of Salatins plus support staff. Living at the farm are Joel's mother Lucille, Joel and his wife Teresa, son Daniel with his wife Sheri, and 3 grandchildren. Employed by the farm are full-time and part-time employees, apprentices, interns, salespeople, and subcontract producers on leased land. Daughter Rachel lives 15 minutes away in Staunton, and is the director of the Beverley Street Studio School.

JUST MATILDA AND ME DOWN ON THE FARM

Joel approaches the topic of time management with his characteristic Big Picture point of view. Rather than getting bogged down in the minutia of squeezing 32 hours of work into a 24 hour day, he steps back and asks a critical question, *"Why are you trying to do it yourself?"*

"The single biggest hurdle that keeps farmers from being able to deal with their workload is their cultish reluctance to hire help", observes Joel. *"They are too independent, payroll is too complicated, they don't have the money...the excuses go on and on".* Everyone has talents and gifts, but most people don't possess all the skills required by the farm business. Honestly assess your strengths, suggests Joel, and bring on people with complimentary skills. On Polyface's payroll, for example, is an accountant, a delivery driver, an inventory manager, and a mechanic.

UGH, PROFITS

The subject of hiring help leads right into another mental logjam Joel has become aware of in his work with new farmers: fear of success. There is an underlying tension and guilt between eeking out a subsistence living and earning a comfortable middle class wage. The sustainable farming movement had its roots in the counterculture movement of the 1960's, when consumerism and wealth were viewed as evil personified.

"*Get over it*", says Joel. "*If you want to farm, jump off the cliff! Scale your operation so you can live above subsistence level*". Sustainability means financial as well as ecological. No one wins if you get sick of pinching pennies and quit farming.

TIME AND MOTION STUDIES

Polyface has a well-established intern program, bringing on eight interns and two apprentices every season. In figuring the best way to train these folks, Joel and Daniel turned to an unlikely source of inspiration: time and motion studies pioneered in the industrial revolution. They analyzed the time required to perform basic farm tasks, thus providing the interns with measurable goals. Some examples are:

- Moving chicken shelters: one every minute
- Collecting and packaging eggs: 90 dozen in one hour
- Eviscerating a chicken: 30 seconds or less
- Loading firewood: fill the trailer in 15 minutes or less

The list is long, reflecting the diversity in Polyface's operation. The system has been very successful from both management and intern's point of view. The expectations are clear to both parties

DAY-TO-DAY LIFE AT POLYFACE

Farmwork can dominate every waking minute of your life and steamroll over your family time if you allow it. The Salatins have found that establishing boundaries and a set routine to each day actually results in more time and higher quality work.

Breakfast and dinner are the bookends to the day. Early morning chores are finished before 7:30 breakfast, then everyone heads out to their day's work. Lunch and breaks are taken as needed: there is no formal midday gathering. Dinner, however, is served at 6:00 pm sharp and marks the end of the workday. The family resists the temptation to go back out and do "just one more thing" before dark. This facilitates a positive work/life balance, with the evenings open for rest, relaxation, hobbies, family time, and socializing. Occasionally after-dinner work is necessary, but not too often.

CONTROLLING CHORES

Defining and limiting chores has been very useful for Polyface. They define a chore as task which is repeated daily at the same time. Feeding and moving chickens is a good example. This takes place first thing every morning. The rule of thumb at Polyface is no more than four hours of chores per day. When it creeps above that, it cuts into time available for other projects. Changes must be made, or there will be a ripple effect on overall productivity. A good example of taking control of chores is when Polyface expanded its egg business. There were two options for housing and moving the additional hens: build more eggmobiles, or utilize electric netting (Feathernets). Eggmobiles would have required daily moves and thus would have added choretime. Feathernets are only moved every three days, so would be folded into ordinary farmwork rather than daily chores. Because the chore load at the time was hovering close to four hours, the decision was to go with Feathernets.

ADVICE FOR NEW FARMERS

Joel Salatin has written a host of books on sustainable farming and related topics. All are relevant and inspirational for new farmers. Check out the Polyface website, http://www.polyfacefarms.com/.

PATCHWORK FARM & GREENHOUSE

Aaronsburg, Pennsylvania
SCOTT AND EDA CASE

Patchwork Farm grows bedding plants, perennials, and organic vegetable transplants for sale in the spring. Through summer and fall, they sell certified organic vegetables at twice weekly farmers markets in Centre County. The 144-acre property has been in the family two generations, with Scott and Eda farming it full-time for the last twenty-four years. The couple has four children, ranging from high schoolers to recent college graduates.

LABOR

Patchwork employs twenty-four people in the height of the growing season, starting at minimum wage and increasing with time and experience. The crew at any one time is a combination of full-time and part-time workers. Their labor pool forms two distinct categories. There is a faithful group of local retirees who works in the greenhouse from the end of February to Memorial Day. Then there are young folks who come to the farm after school, and return during college. Two part-timers are retained through the winter. There are also dedicated positions for staffing the farmers market booths, "the smiling face of Patchwork Farm", says Scott.

DIVIDE AND CONQUER

Scott and Eda have worked out a comfortable and effective division of labor according to their own strengths and interests. In general, Eda runs the greenhouse while Scott oversees field operations. Eda handles payroll and associated deductions. Scott keeps up with the other accounting functions. Eda staffs the market booths and arranges the product display, counting on Scott and his crew to deliver the picked/packed/washed/sorted produce to the right place at the right time. Scott also handles the compliance obligations for organic certifications.

ORGANIZING THE DAY

Scott starts each day with two lists: what needs to be done Today, and what needs to be done Soon. Eda, too, relies on lists. They also keep an enormous calendar on the wall which displays which employees are working at which site. Dovetailed with these entries are family activities and appointments.

Scott always carries a 3x5 index card in his pocket, to write down tasks and ideas which pop up during the day. In the evening, he will transfer these to the appropriate master list.

TECHNOLOGY

Although neither Scott nor Eda embrace technology just for fun, they do utilize it where it supports the business. They pay a consultant to maintain a website and Facebook for the farm. They recently adopted the technology to accept credit cards at farmers markets, a move greatly appreciated by their younger customers.

EMPLOYEE RETENTION

The Case household is a welcoming place both personally and professionally. Everyone eats lunch together up at the house, and Eda makes sure there is enough food to go around. Ice cream with or for lunch is a longstanding summer tradition at Patchwork.

As they were bringing up their children, the Case house became a hospitality hub for meals and overnight guests. Just for fun, Scott and Eda once counted the number of "guest nights" they had in one year. They defined one guest night as one person sleeping over one night. The number was an astonishing 900 'guest nights', or an average of three extra folks per night! "My wife is amazing," says Scott. "She can whip up dinner for a crowd with ten minutes notice".

FAMILY TIME

The Cases do make a concerted effort to separate their private life from their work life. Unless there is an emergency or deadline to crunch, the workday comes to a halt at a civilized hour. Eda makes sure there is dinner on the table, although not at a fixed 'clock' time. Dinner is at Dark:30, she explains. The evening meal forms the boundary between the workday and family time.

ADVICE FOR NEW FARMERS

Although lists form the framework of Patchwork's daily endeavors, Scott's main advice is about _not_ sticking rigidly to a list. You have to be extremely flexible in farming, he cautions. The list is just a starting point. Weather, employee availability, soil conditions, what you see when you get out to the field, mechanical breakdowns: there are endless reasons why you might have to shift your priorities on a moment's notice. You need to be willing and able to make adjustments fast. At the end of the day, what is important is that the revised priorities were accomplished, not the original list. The morning's reality will be different than the evening's. Your days will be difficult and frustrating if you try to stick to a plan regardless of what comes your way.

But, he adds, this is not to say you do things randomly or without a plan. You should always have an overall plan, the Big Picture, and make sure your tasks are in alignment.

PURELY FARM

Pipersville, Pennsylvania
JOANNA AND MARC MICHINI

Marc and Joanna Michini raise pastured hogs, chickens, broilers, egg layers, turkeys, and lamb on a twenty-six-acre rented farm in southeastern Pennsylvania. The couple has one child, four-year old Clover. Purely Farm sells their meat and eggs at several weekly farmers markets, through buying clubs, and restaurants. They process their own chickens throughout the summer, opening the farm for direct sales on pick-up day. In 2013, the couple raised 92 hogs, 200 turkeys, 400 broilers, 25 feeder lambs, and ran 170 egg layers. They raise their hogs from farrow to finish, timing their litters by using Artificial Insemination to provide a continuous supply of pork. The lambs are purchased as weanlings, and finished on Purely Farm pasture. Marc and Joanna are in their 10th year of farming.

LABOR

Except for occasional shifts at a friend's restaurant, Marc and Joanna work solely on the farm. They have no full-time employees. A neighbor helps out 25-30 hours per month.

The duties of farm and home are shared between Marc and Joanna. The day to day livestock management is Marc's responsibility. Of necessity, this also entails machinery repair, maintenance, and building projects. This was unfamiliar territory before Marc went into faming, but he has learned on the job.

With Clover being so young, Joanna's current focus is on home and hearth. Because these activities put her in close proximity to the home office, she also takes charge of the administrative end of the farm business. Bill paying, customer contact, inventory control, updating the mailing list, accounting, banking, running household errands, purchasing supplies, and other mundane but necessary clerical tasks fall on her shoulders. Like many young mothers on farms, she feels tension between farm tasks and domestic duties. "Sometimes I don't feel like a farmer anymore", she reflects, comparing the current demands of farming with the early days of courtship and homesteading.

Simultaneous farmers markets force another division of labor. Marc and Joanna literally go in separate directions when markets occur on the same day.

But not all projects are separate. Two key tasks which Marc and Joanna undertake as a team are chicken processing and sausage-making. These days are scheduled months in advance, and are much looked forward to by Marc and Joanna as well as their customers.

SOLO LIVESTOCK MANAGEMENT

Marc manages the livestock on his own, and that's just the way he likes it. He is both the sole decision-maker and his own labor force. He is highly satisfied with how he manages his time. "I can't believe how well he keeps everything organized", observes Joanna. Marc finds he works best without a written To Do list. He has a fixed plan in his head when he walks out the door in the morning. He accepts that there will not be time for everything on his mental "wish list", but also knows exactly which tasks are most important. He makes adjustments as the realities of the day present themselves.

Marc feels that having just one person in charge of the livestock is a strength of Purely Farm. Close observation is critical to managing livestock. Good decisions can be made and upcoming problems avoided based on subtle behavioral signals. For these reasons, Marc would be reluctant to outsource the daily animal care to an employee.

TECHNOLOGY

The farm does not currently have a website. The topic comes up for discussion periodically, but the couple is so busy with their day to day responsibilities that the thought of tackling a new project fails to gain momentum.

Marc and Joanna both use smart phones, but very differently. Marc prefers to answer it in the field, handle the inquiry, and avoid callbacks. "I check it off the list before it gets on the list," he explains. That works because he is candid about his ability to converse at that moment. He takes the call but explains immediately if he cannot talk at length.

Joanna adopts a different strategy to avoid interruptions in her work and childcare. She relies on voicemail, returning messages in the quiet space at the end of the day.

ADVICE FOR NEW FARMERS

"Don't limit your goals to farm ownership", suggests Marc. If farming is how you want to spend your days, there are other ways to do so. Consider working as a farm manager with a steady paycheck. Marc sees many of these opportunities in his region of southeast Pennsylvania. Investors purchase farms but outsource the day-to-day operations because they live and work elsewhere. They hire a professional farm manager, providing a compensation package and budget.

Both Marc and Joanna emphasize the business side of farming. Know where you are spending money and where you are earning it. Be aware of the profit margins and labor requirements of each enterprise. Don't waste your time on efforts that cost money or only marginally contribute to the bottom line (aka pet projects). On a related note, Marc offers advice for those breeding sows and retaining their own gilts. "Cull for performance, not personality" he says. He has seen far too many new farmers choose and keep sows based on friendliness alone, even when that sow turns out to be a poor producer in the piglet department.

Joanna further suggests that new farmers think ahead to how they will accomplish the clerical tasks on the farm. In a team or couple situation, who wants to take that on? It can't be avoided: everyone can't always be outside doing the fun stuff. If the farm is to be run like a business, certain areas must be handled correctly. Accounting, marketing, regulatory affairs, and payroll are prime examples of specialties which businesses typically outsource.

Marc and Joanna offer a closing thought on the farming lifestyle. It will be rich, eventful, and satisfying, but don't expect it to be immune from problems. Even with being home on the farm, Marc and Joanna struggle with the balance between work life, home life, and enough time with Clover.

QUIET CREEK HERB FARM AND SCHOOL OF COUNTRY LIVING

Brookville, Pennsylvania
THE ORNER FAMILY

Claire and Rusty Orner with their sons, Walker and Ashton, are the stewards of Quiet Creek Herb Farm & School of Country Living. This rolling thirty-acre farm is managed as a 501C non-profit, charitable, educational organization, dedicated to increasing public awareness of conservation, ecological thinking and healthful sustainable living. Rusty and Claire make their entire living from the farm, with no outside income. The three interrelated segments to their business are organic production, education, and a farm store. The bountiful gardens are lush with herbs, vegetables, and flowers. These products fill the on-site gift shop with fresh and dried herbs, herbal teas, vinegars, essential oils, wreaths, soaps, herbal salves, tinctures, mushroom logs, books, and bird and bat houses— all made at Quiet Creek.

Education is a year-round endeavor, with classes ranging

from school field trips to multiple-day summer camps and conferences. Some classes are taught by Rusty and Claire, others by guest speakers. Sustainable living is the common denominator, with topics ranging from basic gardening to renewable energy.

LABOR STRATEGY

Full-time interns are the foundation of Quiet Creek's staff, with additional help dropping in on an hourly or volunteer basis as needed. Interns work for room and board, dining with the family and taking turns cooking. Over forty young people have interned at Quiet Creek over the last fifteen years, and the program is a continuing source of energy, enthusiasm, and creativity

A unique aspect of a Quiet Creek internship is the opportunity to be fully responsible for one aspect of the business. Rusty and Claire fully believe in learning through a sense of ownership. Each intern chooses a farm enterprise for which he is wholly responsible for the season. Examples might be growing a crop such as mushrooms, designing an herb garden, or introducing a new product to the gift shop. Rusty and Claire oversee the project and assist as requested, but the day-to-day work and decisions are left to the intern. Mistakes are considered part of the experience.

SEASONAL SEGMENTATION

Each segment of Quiet Creek's business requires an enormous time commitment and great attention to detail. Scheduling and promoting the educational programs demands organizational skills of the highest order. Stocking and filling the gift shop with hand-made goods takes months of effort. The organic gardens rely on more hand-labor than machine. Rather than tackling these mammoth projects simultaneously, Rusty and Claire parcel them out to different times of the year

Claire schedules the entire year of educational offerings and school field trips in the winter. Her goal is to have the entire season planned by February 1. She also uses the winter months for writing grant proposals and seeking other funding sources consistent with their status as a 501C.

Winter is also the season to fill the on-farm gift shop. It's all hands on deck to produce and package a year's worth of herbal products that will keep the shelves full during the busy season.

Rusty, in the meantime, is in the workshop getting ahead of the curve on maintenance and repairs. Any mechanical work that can be anticipated and completed in the quiet season will save time and frustration during the busy season.

Spring through fall are dedicated to the execution of these winter plans. The farm is abuzz with activity as gardens are tended, field trips hosted, and the gift shop offers its delights.

SPREAD OUT SPRING PLANTING

Rather than one massive undertaking, so-called spring planting at Quiet Creek is actually spread out from February through May. Strategic plantings are made every two weeks, starting in the greenhouse and high-tunnel and graduating to the outside gardens as weather and mud permit. This allows the planting to be integrated with the other spring tasks and spreads the risk of unfavorable conditions.

THE COLOR-CODED CHALKBOARD

With multiple businesses and multiple personnel, organizing who does what presents quite a challenge. Rusty and Claire have figured out a simple yet effective system for planning and tracking the workflow. In the kitchen where everyone shares meals is a large blackboard with the 7 weekdays permanently inscribed. Each family member, children included, and intern is assigned a chalk color. Every Monday, Rusty and Claire craft a plan for the week, writing each task in the color of the responsible person. A staff meeting is held on Tuesday morning to discuss the upcoming week. The genius of the system is its visibility: The board is seen at every meal. Completed items are erased, pending items remain, and adjustments made as needed. No idea is lost: a task stays on the board until it is done.

BALANCING PUBLIC AND PERSONAL TIME

Rusty and Claire have figured out an effective way to strike a balance between family time, fundamental farm work, and public. Quiet Creek is open to the public on Fridays and Saturdays. This means gift shop is staffed, and someone is specifically assigned to greet visitors and give guided tours. The other weekdays are for scheduled field trips, with farm work carried on around that block of time.

USE OF TECHNOLOGY

Rusty and Claire maintain firm control on how far technology is allowed to intrude on their life. They do have a farm website with online ordering capability. They do have wireless access in all the farm buildings. However, the wireless is turned off at night. Early to bed and early to rise is the expectation for all staff members.

Rusty and Claire do not carry cell phones, and do not have an answering machine. There are telephones in gift shop, house, and office. Claire spends about one third of each day on office-based tasks, during which time she is available to answer the phone.

ADVICE FOR NEW FARMERS

Having worked with so many young people as interns, Claire and Rusty have sound advice for those starting out. "Don't be afraid to make mistakes", they suggest. This is consistent with the way they run their intern program. Learn through trial and error. Experiment and see what works for you. Understand that every farm and every farmer is different. Watch what others are doing and look for ideas, but don't expect to mirror other people's techniques and achieve the same outcome.

Start small. Achieve success on a small scale, and grow from there. Rusty and Claire have observed many visitors over the years who see what they have and want to replicate it immediately. However, they overlook the fact that Quiet Creek has been slowly building for sixteen years.

Rusty and Claire speak from experience. When they first bought the farm, they quickly became overwhelmed trying to do too many things all at once. The strategies they employ now and suggest to others are based on those early years.

SPIRAL PATH FARM

Loysville, Pennsylvania
THE BROWNBACK FAMILY

Spiral Path Farm operates a 2200-member vegetable CSA on 255 acres in Perry County. They also have a sizeable wholesale produce business. Terra and Mike Brownback have owned the farm since 1978, and have been certified organic since 1994. For their first fifteen years on the property, the couple raised hogs farrow-to-finish by utilizing existing infrastructure. Their interests later turned to vegetable production, and they dipped their toe in the water with a twenty-two member CSA in 1994. The business flourished, and now employs three generations of Brownbacks and a staff of forty in the high season.

LABOR

It takes a dedicated and well-organized team to orchestrate a CSA as complex as Spiral Path. The membership is a matrix of three membership levels (full, medium or sampler), three time spans (from one month to a full season) and three geographical regions offering up to ten pick-up sites six days a week.

"We think of the organization as spokes on a wheel," describes Terra. She and Mike form the hub of the wheel, overseeing activities which impact the business as a whole. These include ordering supplies, maintaining organic certification, and staffing. The "spokes" on the wheel are greenhouse operations, field grow-out, CSA logistics from picking to packing, trucking, and administration.

Mike Brownback and his adult son Will are in charge of field operations, from seed purchase through harvest and every task in between. Working with them is the greenhouse manager and staff. After the produce is picked, it passes into the jurisdiction of Will's brother Lucas for washing, packing, and delivery. Lucas works at the transplant greenhouses and is the CSA Manager, whose duties include overseeing and working with the packinghouse crew to fill boxes weekly. Full-time truck drivers make deliveries six days a week. Back at headquarters, Terra and her staff handle the office end of things. Taxes are outsourced to a CPA, and the rest of the accounting is done in-house using Quickbooks.

Finding and retaining employees is a major concern at Spiral Path. A full-time staff of forty keeps things running smoothly during the height of the growing season. There is on-site housing for sixteen workers, and the rest are local residents commuting to the farm daily. Most of the seasonal employees are laid off at the end of the growing season, with the hope that they will return in the spring. They qualify to collect unemployment compensation during the winter.

In 2013, Spiral Path made a significant change to its operation which improved both cash flow and employee retention. By investing in high tunnels and additional greenhouse space, the Brownbacks extended their CSA season to span April through December. The shorter unemployment window made it more feasible for their current employees to plan their return.

CSA SOFTWARE SAVES THE DAY

When Spiral Path's CSA was small, spreadsheets and printed newsletters were easy to maintain. Customer accounts, preferences, contact details, delivery routes, and informative newsletters were relatively simple. Then along came the miracle of email. Communication became even easier—for a short while. The larger Spiral Path grew, the more of a burden became membership management. Fortunately, as Spiral Path was expanding and becoming more sophisticated, so was an emerging technology: cloud-based management software designed for CSAs. The Brownback family did their research and decided to give it a try. They chose a company called Farmigo. This has been a huge home run, revolutionizing their CSA logistics, accounting, member tracking, etc. and eliminating what might have interfered with continued growth.

INVESTMENT IN EFFICIENCY

The keyword at Spiral Path is efficiency. With the business relying on so many parallel chains of events, anything that streamlines one operation will benefit others. The Brownbacks do not shy away from investments which improve efficiency. Examples have included a conveyor belt in the packing house, transplanting equipment, seeders, and salad harvesting equipment. Making the financial decision is not always easy, but the benefits quickly justify the expense.

CONSTANT FLOW OF COMMUNICATION

Modern technology has been a blessing to Spiral Path. Theirs is a business in which instant decisions, changes of plan, and vital news must be communicated throughout the day. Even if everyone had time for daily staff meetings (which they don't), there would be changes and updates in the day the minute the meeting adjourned. Smart phones, texts, and email has solved the challenge of instant communication and keeping the right people "in the loop".

ORGANIZING THE DAYS

Despite the size of her organization, Terra's time management principles are short and sweet. "Know what your priorities are throughout the day", she suggests, "and be flexible enough to change them on a moment's notice". She means that literally: in her business, things can indeed change by the minute. List-making does work for her, but only if she remains flexible about the priorities on that list. Crop failures, weather, mechanical problems, staff absences—the list of variables that can instantly change the priorities on a To Do list is extensive.

Terra also believes that stress is a valid factor for prioritizing. The obvious priorities are things that impact production, customer service, and income. However, if something is causing you stress and you can take action to alleviate it, that is a top priority. Stress has a direct impact on longterm health, without which your lists won't matter at all.

VISITOR MANAGEMENT

Drop-in visitors can be a time management challenge for any farmer. Spiral Path solves this problem by offering members-only Open Farm Days once a month. They inform their members ever so tactfully that ordinary days are just too busy to welcome visitors. They even add member benefits to Open Farm Days such as strawberry picking, flower day, and picnics.

ADVICE FOR NEW FARMERS

"Don't worry if you are new to farming", says Terra. She points out that people start farming from all kinds of backgrounds. She and Mike had no farming experience when they bought Spiral Path. She suggests visiting other farms to see how they do things. Farmers are generally very open to helping others.

Your biggest asset are your eyes: observation. Watch carefully what you are growing and raising, and how it responds. You will learn from your crops and livestock.

No matter what size your farm is, be aware of efficiency. Are there tasks which are taking more than their share of time? Can they be done differently? Are there tasks that take too much time, and perhaps do not even fit in with your long-term goals, but are someone's "pet projects"? This is not to say that pet projects are not allowed, but they should be acknowledged and recognized as such.

Think about the size and scale you are aiming for. What size farm feels right to you? This may change and evolve over time, but that is a natural process. Don't dismiss the idea of investing in infrastructure or machinery that can improve your efficiency or extend your labor resources. Beyond a certain scale, you can't do it all yourself without severely limiting your growth.

STEAM VALLEY FIBER FARM

Trout Run, Pennsylvania
PHYLLERI BALL

Over the past fourteen years, Phylleri Ball has built a multi-tiered business raising and marketing wool and mohair. She grazes angora goats and Border Leicester sheep on fourteen owned acres and forty leased. Her signature products are hand-dyed roving, yarn, and handspun socks. She also retails spinning wheels and related equipment, lambskins, books, videos, and finished woolen goods. She teaches dyeing and spinning in her home studio and at fiber events. The demand for her products far exceeds the capacity of her flock, so she buys additional fleeces from othe producers. This adds up to skirting and washing over 100 fleeces a year.

Phylleri sells her products at a number of venues, depending on the season. For eight-ten summer weeks, she runs a booth at a local farmers market. Fall is the season for travelling to major fiber and craft shows, some lasting an entire week. On top of all this, she also maintains an extensive garden, laying hens, and milking goats to sustain her family and interns.

The work at Steam Valley falls roughly into two categories. First comes the livestock: daily chores, fencing, health and hooves, parasite control, breeding, birthing, and facilities management. Then there is the entire hand-dyed, hand-spun fiber business, labor-intensive by design.

Phylleri's life presents two time-management challenges. First, she is the solo family member responsible for the farm. Her children are now grown, and her husband has other interests besides farming. He is always willing to help with heavy lifting and two-man jobs, but the day-to-day operation rest on Phylleri's shoulders. The second challenge is taking care of the farm while on the road at craft shows.

LABOR STRATEGY

Phylleri brings on several interns each year to balance the work load. She has developed a highly organized system for the whole experience, from selection through day-to-day management. Her philosophy is to work as a team with the interns, in a "job shadow" capacity, rather than just handing off all the mindless, repetitive jobs. This approach takes more time, but results in a skilled intern who can handle meaningful responsibilities on the farm. New interns work for room, board, and personalized mentoring. Returning and experienced interns earn a stipend.

It took several years for Phylleri to iron out the wrinkles in the intern program. She requires a minimum commitment of eight weeks, as the first four will be spent mostly in training. She has always held interviews and checked references, but through experience has refined what questions to ask, how to interpret the answers, and how to set realistic expectations for the candidate. Over the years some interns left early, most worked out well, and some became lifelong friends.

USE OF TECHNOLOGY

Steam Valley Fiber Farm has a website, and much of the customer contact is handled through email. Phylleri does not use a cellphone in her business, although she carries one in case of emergency. The landline and answering machine are sufficient for the needs of her business.

TIME MANAGEMENT TIP: WEEKLY PLAN

The interns are off on Sundays, making this a good day for reflection and planning on Phylleri's part. She inspects all areas of the farm, notes corrections to be made, and lays out a plan of work for the upcoming week. A breakfast meeting with the interns starts things out first thing Monday morning.

TIME MANAGEMENT TIP: ON-SITE PASTURE RECORDS

With different people involved in rotating pastures, Phylleri came up with a way of keeping vital information where it is needed: in the field. In each pasture she keeps a journal of grazing history: which animals were last in the paddock, how many head, when they moved on, when they moved off, notes of interest. The journal and writing implements reside in a weather- and bear-proof container (bruins being the reason she runs guard dogs with her goats) next to the fence. This allows the interns to make informed decisions as to where the flock should move next.

TIME MANAGEMENT TIP: FIXED CHORE PATTERNS

Certain seasonal chores have set patterns that create an order out of the rest of the day. When the goats are milking, for example, every day begins in the milking barn at daybreak. That chore repeats itself in the evening. These two bookends establish the discretionary time in between which is available for other projects.

ADVICE FOR NEW FARMERS

There are traits and habits you can develop even before you start farming which are essential to success. Become a good problem-solver. The only thing that is constant on a farm is change. If you throw up your hands in despair every time something goes awry, you will be continually frustrated by farming. Pondering solutions and thinking "out of the box" is part of the game.

Pay attention to the world around you: you need all five senses in farming. From the weather to animal health to growth patterns in the garden—success is in the details.

Expect your life to be dictated by forces outside yourself—weather, seasons, animal health and behavior, plants, even your customers. If you take this as an adversarial relationship, as in "at war with the elements" or "at the mercy of nature", farming will not bring you joy. Being in tune with the ebb and flow will be a more rewarding and less stressful outlook.

You will need to be organized, but this trait can be acquired. Do not despair if you are not a naturally organized person. Phylleri tells how she was quite disorganized in her life before the farm. She endured good-natured teasing from her friends about this character trait. But once she bought the farm, had animals depending on her, and became her own boss, she seized the bit in her teeth and became superbly organized. All it took was the motivation (and yes—now her friends tease her about being too rigid!).

TEWKSBURY GRACE FARM

Muncy, Pennsylvania
JOHN AND LEAH TEWKSBURY

John and Leah Tewksbury produce sustainably grown heirloom vegetables, herbs, fruits, jam, and Shitake mushrooms on twenty-one acres of mixed farmland, open meadows and hardwood forest. They sell through a forty-member CSA and to five restaurants. They do almost all the work themselves, with the help of a once-a-week volunteer. John is a full-time kindergarten teacher while Leah works full-time on the farm.

If this couple had a theme for their farm, it would be "less is more". Leah describes their operation as a "hand-cultivated, non-mechanized, right-sized farm". Their original vision was a farm which could provide a comfortable income without relying on hired help. This they have achieved. Their CSA fills to capacity every year and maintains a waiting list.

FREEDOM FROM MACHINERY

Absence of power equipment is a distinguishing feature of Tewksbury Grace Farm. John and Leah do not own a tractor, rototiller, or other farm machinery. Nor do they use draft horses. Planting, weeding, cultivating, and harvesting are all done by hand. The crops are grown in raised beds, which reduce weed pressure and ergonomically simplify manual tasks. No machinery means less capital outlay, fuel, parts, repairs, maintenance, and unplanned downtime due to mechanical breakdown.

KEEPING TECHNOLOGY IN ITS PLACE

Modern technology plays a minimal role at Tewksbury Grace Farm. The CSA is filled to capacity, and neither Leah nor John enjoy working at the computer. Since they are not seeking to expand their operations for increased sales, they do not spend time on marketing activities except for a basic listing in www.localharvest.org. They do not have a farm website, use Facebook, keep a blog, or advertise. Neither John nor Leah carries a cell phone, finding them to be a distraction and time-waster. The telephone and answering machine are in the house, and calls are returned as promptly as possible. "It drives our family and friends crazy" confesses Leah, "but it works for us". Computers are used for record-keeping, email, research, and education. They acknowledge that certain technologies can be useful and increase efficiencies; if they were looking to increase their sales/customer base, then using social media networks or a website would be helpful recruiting and advertising outlets.

SAVING TIME BY STAYING HOME

Living forty-five minutes away from the nearest city, Leah and John are keenly aware of how quickly a day gets chewed up when they leave the farm to run errands. When they were new to farming, the couple helped start the Susquehanna Valley Growers Market and participated in it weekly. After a few years, they left the market, and began offering CSA shares as their customer base grew. "There is a day and night difference in the amount of time and energy required to grow the same amount of food", explains Leah. "Traveling to the farmer's market was very labor-intensive. It is actually more efficient for us to deliver the CSA shares than to go to market". And that is just what they do. Every Friday is dedicated to delivering CSA shares and restaurant orders as well as miscellaneous household errands.

DAILY, WEEKLY, SEASONAL SCHEDULES

There is a set pattern which organizes each day, week, and season. The morning begins with a weather update and revised plan for the day. John and Leah pull out yesterday's To Do list and make necessary changes. The Scheduling Book is consulted. This is the official "diary" of what has ever been planted, grown, and harvested plus significant notes and insights.

On Tuesdays, they evaluate the harvest and plan the contents of the weekly CSA shares. Wednesday and Thursday are dedicated to harvesting and processing. The restaurants are notified of what they will be receiving so they can plan their menus. Friday is delivery day. Saturday through Monday is open for farm projects and recreation.

Thanksgiving marks the end of the CSA year, and everything starts up again in April. There are no winter crops or season-extension programs. John and Leah value the time to rest and recharge in the winter. They catch up on record-keeping, analyze the numbers, and research new projects. A highlight of each winter is their personal "Farm Summit", when the couple reviews the results of the previous year and works in new ideas going forward.

INVESTING IN QUALITY

Just because John and Leah do not buy power equipment does not mean they are free from capital investment. They use a highly efficient, low-cost Coolbot refrigeration system. For the greenhouse, they paid top dollar for heat mats and the greenhouse building plastic, which perform well and last season after season. They also invest wisely and carefully in hand tools. Being a non-mechanized farm, John and Leah find high-quality, ergonomically correct tools to be essentials. They last longer and perform better than cheap, mass-produced items.

ADVICE FOR NEW FARMERS

Visit as many different farming operations as you can, suggests Leah, and pay attention to the details. You never know what ideas and observations will turn out to be useful on your own farm. From a practical standpoint, she strongly advises investing in a good refrigeration system as soon as possible. This is the foundation of a successful produce operation. It allows you to maintain the quality of your product while manipulating the timing between harvest and sale. The second important investment is irrigation. Refrigeration and irrigation are critical early investments in produce operations.

Tewksbury Grace Farm stands as a role model for one of the founding principals of success in life: don't do things just because others are doing it. John and Leah's farm stands out from the crowd with its lack of power machinery, single-family size, and minimal reliance on technology. That model may not work for everyone, but it certainly works for them.

STRYKER FARM

Saylorsburg, Pennsylvania
NOLAN THEVENET

Nolan Thevenet is the young twenty-something owner and operator of Stryker Farm, a forty-seven-acre property in the Poconos mountains. Nolan raises heritage pigs, goats, and laying hens. Diversity is the hallmark of his marketing efforts. He sells to stores, restaurants, and buying clubs as well as direct to consumers. He attends farmers markets. He is just gearing up to offer online shipping for his meats.

LABOR

Nolan has worked full-time on the farm since 2010. He does not currently employ full-time help. He does have a neighbor who can work on an as-needed basis. Nolan's mother lives on the farm as well, and she is happy to help when needed. There have been a couple of summer interns, but no plan to make that an annual ritual.

NUMBERED TO DO LIST

Nolan wears many hats. On a typical day, he in charge of 120 pigs, fifty goats, 400 laying hens, and two guard dogs. Facilities and customer service also require his attention. Nolan relies on a written list to get the right things done, numbering by priority. The list undergoes multiple edits throughout the day. When he has help, Nolan delegates tasks that do not need his personal input, such as collecting and washing eggs. There are three areas, however, which he prefers to handle personally even though it does increase his workload: customer service, website design, and daily livestock chores.

Stryker Farm customers form a relationship with Nolan, and he is the one with whom they prefer to communicate. This gives him control over critical details.

The farm website is programmed by a designer, but Nolan provides input on the content and functionality.

Even if he did have full-time help, Nolan would not outsource the daily livestock care. Observation and detail are critical to his pasture-based farrow to finish operation. Subtle behaviors invisible to the untrained eye can reveal developing health problems. Litters arriving in the wrong place at the wrong time constitute a "drop everything" emergency. Even the sounds of the herd can point to something as important as a malfunctioning waterer.

STRYKER FARM TECHNOLOGY

Modern technology is the key to Nolan's success in running this diversified farm almost single-handedly. His website serves as both a guided tour and an order-taker. Customers can print off order forms for meat packages. The online Farm Store which is currently under development will even offer real-time order-taking. Nolan communicates with customers and suppliers via email, texting, and phone calls using an IPhone. "I am bombarded with phone calls all day", he observes.

The administrative tasks of the business also take a great deal of time. Nolan uses his home office for bookkeeping, marketing, scheduling processing dates and pick-ups, ordering feed and supplies, and the countless other clerical tasks which keep the farm humming. He puts in at least one block of office time a day in the morning, evening, or both.

ADVICE FOR NEW FARMERS

If you are starting up a new farm, expect it to take all the time you have available. "You will be working three times as hard as your non-farming friends, to make half the money", quips Nolan. But on a serious note, he strongly suggests setting long-term goals to give meaning to the hard work and long hours. This is exactly what keeps Nolan going week after long week.

Nolan typically works fourteen- hour days. He rarely takes a day off. Nor does he have a slack season in the winter like some operations, because his marketing channels demand product all year round. But he does not resent the workload, because he is making progress towards a five-year goal. He is expanding his customer base and improving his infrastructure to the point where he can afford to hire a full-time employee. That will enable Nolan to take more time off and balance his life with other activities and interests in addition to the farm.

WYNNORR FARM

Westtown Township, Pennsylvania
JOE AND LAURA STRATTON

Joe and Laura are the third generation to live and work on Wynnorr Farm, which has been in the family since 1924 and is one of the last working farms in Westtown Township.

Their mission is to keep the farm in Production Agriculture while educating the public about the science and business of farming. They operate several integrated enterprises to support these goals.

The land is mostly dedicated to growing produce and a flock of Dorset sheep. They run a retail stand at the farm, and are widely known for their sweet corn and tomatoes. Yarn and sheepskins from the flock and items produced by neighboring farms round out the selection. The store is open seven days a week from June through October.

The Strattons also offer a CSA in partnership with eight nearby Amish farms. Together, they offer shareholders a wide variety of produce and homemade goods in a twenty-four week subscription from May through October. The weekly pick-up is at Wynnorr Farm.

Fall is the season for "agritainment" at Wynnorr. Visitors

can go through a corn maze, take a hay ride, pedal go-karts, try an apple toss, or pick their own pumpkins. The farm stand brims with seasonal specialties like apple cider and pies. Visitors range from school bus tours to individual families.

On top of all this, Joe works part-time off the farm and runs a consulting business for small farms.

Joe and Laura share management responsibilities and hands-on work. Laura is in charge of hiring, payroll, scheduling, customer communications, and the CSA. Joe handles all the field work and the mechanical end of things.

LABOR STRATEGY

The common denominator to all these enterprises is staffing. The field work, farmstand, CSA, and guest services all depend on a team of skilled people working in parallel. For Joe and Laura, this is not a problem: it is an opportunity. They feel strongly that part of their mission on the farm is to create opportunities for young people. That is why the staff consists largely of teenagers or college students.

Hiring this age group can be challenging because of limited availability. As enthusiastic as a teen may be about his first job, his availability is whittled away by school, sports, and family time. Rather than view this situation as an obstacle, Joe and Laura simply factor it into their system. They hire 25 people every summer, planning for 6 to be working on any given day. To create the schedule, Laura uses a web-based employee scheduling software called WhenToWork[SM].com. She enters her staffing needs and the employees enter their availability and preferences. There is even a feature for last-minute shift exchanges. The software crunches all this data, proposes a schedule, and notifies all interested parties. To do this by hand used to take Laura an entire day. Now it takes just a morning to review and authorize the proposed schedule.

For most of their employees, working at Wynnorr is their first job. Joe and Laura strive to make it a positive experience where the young person can gain skills that extend beyond farming. Leadership skills are cultivated by designating team leaders. Shifts are kept to four hours or less. Joe and Laura try very hard not to micromanage the staff, and to increase responsibilities as skills and initiative allow.

The Strattons also employ a part-time bookkeeper. The paperwork generated from multiple businesses and a large staff justifies the time and expertise of an accountant.

USE OF TECHNOLOGY

The WhenToWork^{sm} software is the most important technological tool on the farm, followed closely by the farm's website. Joe and Laura carry smartphones, and find the web access to be a great timesaver. Web-based queries or projects do not have to wait for office time.

CONSISTENT SCHEDULES

Multiple, time-sensitive business occurring simultaneously—seems like a disaster waiting to happen. But Joe and Laura create order out of potential chaos by observing strict schedules each week and each day. Each workday starts half an hour before the farm stand opens, with a casual staff meeting on the patio. The team reviews the plan for the day and any pertinent news or announcements. Changes of shift occur the same time every day, as does closing time. Tuesday and Friday are dedicated to the CSA: harvesting, cleaning, packing, and distribution. A newsletter goes out to shareholders twice a week like clockwork. The farm stand and visitor activities operate on a set schedule throughout the season. The exception is farm tours, which occur at random times but are scheduled in advance.

WHAT'S THE MOST IMPORTANT THING RIGHT NOW?

Joe is not a list-maker. When he has discretionary time not dictated by outside forces, he asks himself one question. "What is the single most important thing I should do right now?" The answer usually pops up immediately. It is likely to be a time-sensitive task: seeds to plant, equipment to fix, a task to accomplish before bad weather sets in. Limiting the choice to one allows the most important thing to rise to the top of his mind, rather than spinning a fantasy of the 15 things he would like to do before the sun sets.

PREVIOUS TIME MANAGEMENT EXPERIENCE

Joe brings to the farm an extensive formal background in time management. His business and consulting career included professional training with the Franklin Covey Co, a world leader in organizational products and techniques integrated with leadership training. This company is best known for the book "The Seven Habits of Highly Effective People", ranked by Time Magazine in 2011 as one of <u>25 Most Influential Business Management books.</u>

Joe's approach to time management is to begin with the mission and vision, then fill in the necessary supporting projects and details. He guides the family in creating this "Big Picture" and ensuring that the daily tasks align with the long-term goals.

ADVICE FOR NEW FARMERS

"Don't wait too long!" advises Joe. He meets aspiring farmers all the time with his consulting business, and his most popular workshop is "Building Your Small Farm Dream". Young people naturally have more energy and more appetite for risk than older folks. The sooner the better, he believes, rather than waiting for some imagined perfect time in the future when circumstances are "just right".

Joe and Laura are also big believers in trial periods. They encourage young people to try their hand at farming under someone else's guidance before going out on their own.

"Work for more than one farm", suggests Joe. "Go beyond what you think you are interested in, and get experience with different types of farming". Joe has even encouraged some of his best long-term employees to work at neighboring farms to broaden their experience.

Another option is to "test-drive" a project on someone else's farm. Joe and Laura have allowed numerous young folks to raise livestock or crops on their farm. Wynnorr provides the site, and the new farmer is solely responsible for the project. "Start small," adds Laura. "Grow into your products and services at a scale where you can do them well".

The Connection between Holistic Management and Time Management

BY ANN ADAMS

Many people have heard about Holistic Management and are excited about the results ranchers and farmers are getting on their land and in their bank accounts with this adaptive management process. While those results are indeed exciting, equally exciting is the results these agricultural producers are getting in their quality of life (the social leg of the sustainability stool). Because Holistic Management helps managers to manage for the triple bottom line of profit, people, and the planet, the focus is to make sure all legs of that sustainability stool are strong. If one is weak then the whole stool is not strong or resilient.

So what is Holistic Management and how does it help people improve their quality of life? Let's look at the results that people have achieved as noted in post training surveys. Holistic Management practitioners have experienced the following human resource management results:

Result	% of respondents who experienced result
Clearer sense of what your farm/ranch is managing towards	100%
More efficient use of resources	81%
Improved communication on the farm/ranch	69%
Improved decision-making	92%
Improved efficiency of farm/ranch chores	57%

When we look at how Holistic Management helps people accomplish these results, we can see below in figure 1 the "kernel" of Holistic Management is the holistic goal. This decision making tool helps people not only articulate their key values, but helps them make decisions consistently toward those values. Does that sound easy? On a scale of 1-10, how would you rate your operation and your management to provide the quality of life articulated by the management team? If you think there is room for improvement, read on.

The Principles

Let's start with the basics. Holistic Management is based on two key principles:

1. Nature functions in wholes
2. Understand your environment

The first principle focuses on the idea of holism, helping us to shift our paradigm to focus on building symbiotic relationships in all our management decisions. We have to pay attention to the relationships between the different aspects of the whole. Anytime you change one thing, it impacts other areas of your life. We keep that in mind with Holistic Management by using a holistic goal to help us keep focused on the big picture and reduce unintended consequences.

If you focus your management time on building those symbiotic relationships rather than just doing what you've been doing, then you are more likely to get more results for less work. Think of the 80/20 rule. 20% of what you do yields 80% of the results you achieve. If you figure out what that 20% is, you make better use of the time you have. The key to the 80/20 rule is building symbiotic relationships (people, animals, soil, plants, etc.).

The second principle is to help people focus on understanding that all tools do not have the same effect in different environments. With this principle we remember that there are no one size fits all solutions. What may be a "best management practice" in one area of the world could cause problems in another area. Moreover, what is considered a standard management practice (ie. Calving in January), may actually be a huge time suck. Taking time to understand how you can partner with Nature rather than fight it will reduce a lot of stress and wasted time.

with Nature — one size does NOT fit all

The Practices

Now let's look at the six key steps to practicing Holistic Management:

1. Define what you manage
2. State what you want
3. Aim for healthy soil
4. Consider all tools
5. Test your decisions
6. Monitor your results

Practice One—Define what you manage

Define what you manage is looking at the *inventory* that you are managing. The two key areas of that inventory to define are your *management team* (decision makers) and your *assets*. When defining the management team you focus on who is making management decisions at the various levels of managements. Those people are the ones that should help create a holistic goal and who must have ownership in it, because if they don't, you'll have a hard time making progress toward this. Likewise, not having the right person doing the right job is another sure way to waste time and effort.

All your *assets* would include clients and vendors, tangible assets like buildings, equipment, and livestock, and money as well as less tangible assets like skills and knowledge. Knowing what your inventory is then allows you to better manage it. This step can make you further aware of the influences impacting the inventory that you manage and how you affect them. Again, think of the 80/20 rule.

Practice Two—State what you want

Working with your other decisions makers on your management team, begin the process of creating your holistic goal—describing the life you want to live, based on your deepest values. To create your holistic goal, ask your management team to describe:

1. The quality of life desired (Quality of Life)
2. What to create or produce to live that life (Behaviors, Systems, & Processes)
3. What must exist to sustain that life in the future (Vision)

These three different pieces of a holistic goal help the team define the quality of life they want right now which motivates them to manage toward the common ground articulated, more effectively focusing on the priorities at hand for the greater good of the family or business rather than individual interests. It also helps them identify the behaviors, systems, and processes they must put in place to get there (which includes the various plans necessary for prioritizing action). Lastly, it helps them articulate their vision for the future with the legacy they want to leave in regards to their relationships with their communities and the land by describing:

1. How you have to behave
2. The future landscape
3. The future community

4. In this way the holistic goal provides guidance for both short and long-term decision-making, setting priorities at every step of the way.

Practice Three—Aim for healthy soil

This practice uses four fundamental ecosystem processes in Nature, so you can begin to assess the health of your land and consider it in your management decisions. The four ecosystem processes are:

1. Water cycle
2. Mineral cycle
3. Energy Flow
4. Biological communities

The earliest indicator of ecosystem health is soil cover and soil health. If there is 100% soil cover, made up of living and decaying plants and a great diversity of species, you likely have a healthy environment. If not, your production plans must keep you moving toward producing healthier soil to build resilience in your land and in your business.

Practice Four—Consider all tools available

The tools for managing ecosystem processes fall into six broad categories:

1. Human Creativity
2. Technology
3. Rest

  4. Fire ?
  5. Animals and Living Organisms
  6. Money & Labor

Human creativity and money and labor are required in using the other tools. In land management, fire, rest, and technology are the most used tools to modify our ecosystem. However, the impact from animals and living organisms can help improve land health, water infiltration, and the land's ability to sequester carbon through grazing and animal impact by many different species for a great deal less money—and more symbiotic relationships reduce time/labor and inputs that don't pay for themselves.

Tools are neither good nor bad and should be managed within the context of the whole under management. Consider your holistic goal and the degree of brittleness of the environment you manage, along with other factors before you decide whether or not a particular tool is suitable.

Practice Five—Test your decisions

The seven Holistic Management testing questions help us sift through the many factors and complex variables to get to the heart of the matter and help improve decision-making and prioritizing actions. Ultimately, we are looking at whether the action or decision meets the triple bottom line you have articulated in your holistic goal. These seven tests supplement other considerations when making a decision (research, intuition, cash flow, etc.). The seven tests are:

1. *Root Cause*—Does this action address the root cause of the problem?
2. *Weak Link*
    a. *Social*—Are there any social concerns regarding this action?
    b. *Biological*—Does this action address the weakest point in the life cycle of this organism?
    c. *Financial*—Does this action address the weakest link in the chain of production? In my enterprise, what single thing will have the greatest positive impact on my chain of production?
3. *Comparing Options*—Which action gets the "biggest bang for the buck" toward your holistic goal? Where is your highest return?
4. *Gross Profit Analysis*—Which enterprises contribute most to cover the fixed costs (overhead) of the business?
5. *Input Analysis*—Is the energy or money to be used in this action derived from the most appropriate source in terms of your holistic goal? Will the way the energy or money is to be used lead toward your holistic goal?
6. *Vision Analysis*—Does this action lead toward or away from the Vision articulated in your holistic goal?
7. *Gut Check*—Considering all the testing questions and your holistic goal, how do you feel about this action or decision now?

You may test decisions individually on a day-to-day basis or you will make higher level decisions as part of your strategic plan that will be based in your financial planning, biological monitoring, land planning, or grazing planning (or other production planning you do). All of these plans require clear management plans that guide how you spend your time.

Practice Six—Monitor your results

Before you begin to implement a decision, consider any unintended consequences that could arise from your actions. Determine the earliest warning signs that might say you're going off track. Monitor those indicators carefully; take action if things start to go wrong or circumstances change. The sooner you respond, the less time and money is wasted.

To learn more about Holistic Management, visit HMI's website: www.holisticmanagement.org.

MAXIMIZE OUTREACH, MINIMIZE TIME WITH A WEEKLY COMMUNICATION SCHEDULE

A 3-Part Series Originally Published on SmallFarmCentral.com
By Simon Huntley

Have you ever been stumped on what to write to your email list? Or what to post to your Facebook page? Do your other duties as a farmer, farmers market manager, or CSA manager overwhelm your ability to communicate with your online audience about what you are doing? You are busy and marketing often falls to the bottom of the pile. I get that. I've been there.

However, if customers don't show up to buy what you sell, the numbers will not add up and you will not be able to sustain your farm or farmers market in the long term. I want you to thrive over the next 5 to 10 years and marketing is one of the pillars of that success!

In a series of three articles, I will help you build a weekly communication strategy that is defined, consistent, and repeatable. I am not going to focus on how you attract new online interest. I am going to focus on how to engage with the people who have already opted in to follow you so you can turn them from followers into customers and encourage repeat business.

By using my blueprint to create your own plan, you will reduce your stress during the busy time while maximizing your outreach potential. During two hours of scheduled "marketing time" each week, you will develop a few key pieces of content and schedule that content to go out at the right time during the week so you can focus on farming and managing rather than tweeting and emailing.

In this first part, you will learn what pieces of content you need to create each week. This will take you an hour or less each week. In the second part, you will learn how to choose your communication channels. In the third part, I will give you an editable schedule for your weekly communication and show you how to use technology to schedule all of your communication ahead of time so the technology does the work for you! The final goal is for you to have an actionable process that you can execute on throughout your season.

Part 1: The Three Pieces of Content You Need to Create Each Week

To create a weekly communication schedule to maximize your outreach and sales, the first step is to figure out what to post! If you need to come up with a new concept for your posts each week, you will fail during the busy season. It is just too much mental effort to come up with something creative each week.

Understand that your customers are reading your emails and social media updates on the go while they are in line at the bank or taking a short break from work to click around. They are not in the mood to read 1,000 word novelettes on onion harvesting. I'm happy to say that there is a short cut!

Photos. Look down your Facebook feed. Which posts have the most likes, comments, and shares? They have compelling photos attached. Photos connect customers and would-be customers immediately to your farm, even if they are in line at the bank.

ONE PHOTO, ONE PARAGRAPH

My recommendation is that the raw material of your marketing efforts is a type of post I call "One Photo, One Paragraph". Choose a great photo from the past week (because you are taking photos all the time, right?) or from your archives, write 250 words or less about that photo, and this content goes out on all of your communication channels.

Not only does the photo connect people to the farm, this kind of update is so easy to create. It should not take more than 15 minutes of your time to put this together. Efficiency is of great importance when you are busy.

RECIPE OF THE WEEK

In addition to your photographic masterpiece, pick a recipe of the week that features a product that is for sale or in the CSA box or at market during that week.

Remember, many of your customers are a little nervous in the kitchen and your guidance is essential for success with what they buy. In general, people don't cook much anymore. According to the USDA, food dollars spent outside of the home has gone from 25% to 47% between 1970 and 2012. This is a trend that will not stop soon.

Find a recipe that is simple and easy to prepare. Focus on adaptable recipes that can be prepared in under 30 minutes. Think about teaching good cooking technique rather than impressive culinary creations. Over time, the goal is to build customers that are comfortable improvising in the kitchen.

There are a million sites to find recipes and don't be afraid to repeat a recipe from past seasons. We have posted some of these recipes at 40 Simple and Delicious Recipes which you can use as a resource if you are stumped.

Try to use a recipe that you have prepared or has been recommended by a customer so you can relate your personal experience.Don't spend too much time on this step. Again, this should not take more than 15 minutes. Just think about which product you want to feature that week and go find a simple, delicious recipe that includes it.

SPECIFIC CONTENT FOR MARKETS OR CSA

Depending on your marketing channels, you may want to write a short update specific to CSA members about what is going to be in the box or what is going to be at the farmers market. This content will be used in your CSA or farmers market specific communications.

Spend no more than 15 minutes on this step.

Schedule Time for your Marketing

So far, we have 45 minutes blocked out for you to write a "One photo, one paragraph" update, choose a recipe, and create specific content for sales channels.

For success with this method, it is absolutely essential that that you make the time for this each and every week. I suggest blocking two hours total in your schedule each week and put it on your calendar. There will be times when the pigs get out and you just can't get the exact time to make this happen, but if it is on the calendar, it will happen more often than not.

You are probably wondering why I suggest blocking off two hours instead of just the 45 minutes I have already accounted for. Right now, all you have is the raw material of your communication for the week. We still need to get this out to your followers.

Part 2: Reach People Where They Are

To ensure maximum reach with the least amount of effort on your part, I recommend posting this content to your website, email list, and social media. Some small changes will need to be made for each communication medium, but now that you have the raw content material it should not take more than 30 minutes to repurpose the content and get it ready to go.

Website / Blog

The center of your marketing efforts is your website. Very few people will come to your website independently for the purpose of learning what is new with your farm, but each update you push out should link the reader back your website so they can learn more about you and hopefully buy from you!

For posting this kind of weekly update, posting to a blog within your website is natural. Even if you don't have a blog on your website, you can simply create new pages to house the weekly content. However, any modern website platform including Wordpress or Small Farm Central will make it easy to have a blog within your website.

Another side benefit of having the content on your website is that it will be indexed by search engines so your old blog posts may draw some search engine traffic over the long term.

When you create your email list and your social media posts, link back to the blog article URL. For anyone who is new to your farm or farmers market, they can click on the link and learn more about you on your website and even opt-in to get future communications from you! This is an opportunity to grow your audience and sales over time.

Email List

A robust email list is at the center of your outreach. If you do nothing else for your marketing, create an email mailing list.

Email has been around since 1993. It is the old geezer as far as marketing is concerned. It is not fun and new like social media, but since most people check their email daily, if not constantly through the day, it is a very powerful tool to reach your audience.

The weekly email needs to be short and punchy. Remember, many people are checking this on their phone with a tiny screen and in the middle of the rest of their busy lives. Just add your "One photo, one paragraph" at the top of the email, then your weekly recipe, and then anything else people need to know to buy from you (for example where you will be at market that week).

Use an email marketing tool like Mailchimp (which can work in conjunction with Small Farm Central's email tools), Constant Contact, Drip, or any of the hundreds of other ones out there. This allows you to gather stats, like open rates and click through rates, but it also keeps your emails out of spam folders. Any email marketing software will also allow recipients to unsubscribe at any time, which is really important to make sure you are not bugging your customer base!

Don't send emails through your regular emailing program. It is not classy or effective.

Segment your lists as much as possible based on what is important in your business. For example, if you sell at multiple markets, make sure you collect information about which market each subscriber is interested in and mark that in your email marketing software. This allows you to send specific communications at the right time to people interested in each market.

Let people opt-in for the mailing list on your website and anywhere you connect with the public, like a farmers market. A key goal in your marketing plan should be to grow your email list over time, so commit to talking up the value of the email list with customers. An email mailing list opt in should be prominent on your website. In fact, short of buying something, opting in to your mailing list is a key goal for any visitor on your website.

Once someone has signed up for your email list, you can nurture them over time and turn them from "interested" into "customer".

Social Media

I think that social media does have a place in your marketing strategy, but I am wary of the time and skill it takes to do right. It is not going to solve your marketing problems all by itself. It is just a part of a successful marketing strategy.

You can spend your whole day marketing your farm or farmers market on social media. If you want to spend hours a day with these tools, that's fine. You will have a whole different approach than I suggest here. I am talking here to people who have many other responsibilities, so I want you to get the most return out of the least amount of time.

I will briefly mention the four main social media platforms of our day: Facebook, Twitter, Instagram, and Pinterest. The social media world is constantly changing. Keep learning to make sure you get the most out of it.

The most effective social media platform that I have seen for farms and farmers markets is Facebook. It is fairly easy to master and it has a huge reach.

There is a lot of talk about Twitter. From my experience, I see few farms using Twitter effectively because it takes a pretty huge time investment to get right. If you want to have a basic account on Twitter, you can simply post your weekly content here and do nothing more with it. You probably won't get a huge reach, but you will reach people who use Twitter as the center of their digital lives.

Instagram, now with 400 million users, has more users than Twitter. I honestly have not delved into Instagram very much yet, so I can't give a whole lot of advice here. I am still watching Instagram to see where it goes. It is very photo based, so it fits well into the strategy I have already laid out here

Pinterest is another popular platform. This is a good place to gather recipes over time into a recipe board, but it is not a platform I can recommend unless you have a really specific interest in it.

If you want to keep it really simple, just make sure you have an active Facebook presence and you can ignore the rest of the social media networks for now!

Text Messages

A great tool, especially for farmers market sales, is the text message. Text messages have a super high open rate (80%+) and are read very quickly after they are sent. They also have a huge reach since anyone with a cell phone can receive text messages — they don't need the latest name brand smartphone to get them!

Physical Copies

Some folks provide physical copies of the newsletter for CSA members or at the farmers market. This can be another way to reach more people, but you will have to balance the cost and time investment to get these printed each week.

Part 3: Schedule, Timing, and Tools:

During your marketing time, use the scheduling tool I detail here (Hootsuite) to schedule these updates to go out automatically during the week. That way, you can focus on growing, harvesting, and everything else you need to do rather than social media updates!

A SAMPLE SCHEDULE:

This example schedule is for a Thursday CSA delivery and a Saturday farmers market. You will make the proper adjustments for your particular scenario.

Monday
1. Develop your content as described in Part 1:
   » One Photo, One Paragraph
   » Recipe of the week
   » Specific content for Markets or CSA
2. Combine this content into a single update and post it on your website/blog. Remember from Part 2, that in general, people will not be refreshing your website to look for new content but we will drive them there with email.
3. Draft emails for your mailing lists and customize them as needed for your CSA members and your market customers. You may have two mailing lists for these segments. The email should not be all of what you just posted but instead should be a compelling teaser outlining what they are going to see when they click through to your site. Don't forget to include that link!

4. Schedule your emails. CSA email will go out Wednesday and/or Thursday. Market email will go Friday.
5. Build your One Photo, One Paragraph content into a social media post. This should mostly just be copying and pasting.
6. Build your Recipe of the week into a social media post. Again, just repurposing the content.
7. Build your Market info into a social media post.
8. Schedule One Photo, One Paragraph to go out Monday on social media (and Wednesday if using Twitter).
9. Schedule Recipe of the week to go out Tuesday on social media (and Thursday if using Twitter).
10. Schedule Market info to go out Friday and/or Saturday on social media.

If you're able to schedule all of these to be automated, you should now be pretty much done for the week. If not, that's not a problem. Even scheduled social media posts and email drafts can be edited. So, even though you have created a lot of content, for today all that goes out is:

- One Photo, One Paragraph posted to social media.

Tuesday
- Recipe of the week posted to social media.

Wednesday
- CSA Email goes out to members telling them what is in the box for tomorrow.

- If using Twitter, One Photo, One Paragraph is tweeted again. Twitter users need to be caught "in the moment" to see your posts so you needn't worry about "spamming" with Twitter.

Thursday
- If needed for your customers, CSA Email goes out to members as a final reminder to get their box.
- If using Twitter, Recipe of the week is tweeted again.

Friday
- Market Email goes out to Saturday farmers market customers goes out 24 hours before market with reminder and product availability.
- Market info posted to social media.

Saturday
- If needed for your customers, last minute market info posted to social media.

Take the time now to write out your own weekly schedule based on your needs using this schedule as an example.

SCHEDULING TOOLS

There are many tools out there to help you schedule your social media updates, but the one I recommend for a farmer or market manager is Hootsuite.

You can start a free account to connect in up to three social networks. If you go beyond that, it is $10/month.

With Hootsuite, you can schedule an update to go out to multiple networks, including Facebook, Twitter, and Instagram, so you can quickly set up a schedule like I have outlined above.

REVIEW ANALYTICS OVER TIME

On a monthly or seasonal basis, review your open rate on your emails, Facebook insights, and Twitter analytics.

This will give you an idea of what content your customers respond to and you should further refine your approach based on the feedback you get from the analytics.

Now that you know what to post, where to post, and when to post it, it important to build this into your weekly routine and execute every week!

Simon Huntley founded Small Farm Central in 2006 to serve the technology needs of over 1,000 small farmers, farmers markets, and other local foods businesses. Services include website builder, CSA member management, online sales technology, and text messages for farmers markets. Simon believes in helping farms reach economic sustainability by any means necessary! More information, including lots of free resources, is available at smallfarmcentral.com

efficiency
in proper technology

...ing
in seeder
Inventory control Real-time

Also prioritize whatever is causing STRESS.

holisticmanagement.org